MPRE Study Guide

Study Outlines for the Multistate Professional Responsibility Examination

AmeriBar

Phone (800) 529-2651 • Fax (800) 529-2652

MPRE Study Guide

TABLE OF CONTENTS

BAR REVIEW COURSES...i
MPRE BASICS AND STRATEGIES ix
Review Questions xiii

I. REGULATION OF THE LEGAL PROFESSION............................1
  A. Powers of Courts and Other Bodies to Regulate Lawyers 1
    1) EXPRESS AUTHORITY 1
    2) INHERENT AUTHORITY 1
      a) Officer of the Court...1
      b) Professional Liability Standards 1
      c) Additional Methods of Exercising Inherent Authority 2
  B. Admission to the Profession 2
    1) BAR ADMISSION 2
      a) False Statements or Nondisclosures...................................3
  C. Regulation After Admission..3
    1) ACTIONS SUBJECTING ATTORNEY TO DISCIPLINE.............3
      a) Violating the Rules 3
        (1) Lawyer's Acts...3
        (2) Acts of Others..3
      b) Criminal Actions...3
      c) Actions Involving Dishonesty...3
    2) DISCIPLINARY MATTERS 3
      a) Lawyer's False Statements or Nondisclosures 3
  D. Mandatory and Permissive Reporting of Professional Misconduct.................4
    1) REPORTING PROFESSIONAL MISCONDUCT 4
      a) Lawyer and Lawyer 4
      b) Lawyer and Judge 4
      c) Exceptions...4
    2) WHAT CONSTITUTES PROFESSIONAL MISCONDUCT 4
  E. Unauthorized Practice of Law 5
    1) UNAUTHORIZED PRACTICE OR ASSISTANCE OF UNAUTHORIZED
      PRACTICE OF LAW 5
  F. Multijurisdictional Practice of Law 5
    1) ASSOCIATION WITH LAWYER IN OTHER JURISDICTION.................5
    2) TRIBUNAL PROCEEDING 6
    3) ALTERNATIVE DISPUTE RESOLUTION PROCEEDING...........6
    4) OTHER CIRCUMSTANCES..6
  G. Fee Division with a Non-Lawyer 6
  H. Law Firm and Other Forms of Practice 7
  I. Responsibility of Partners, Managers, Supervisory and Subordinate Lawyers...7
    1) LAW FIRMS AND ASSOCIATIONS...7
      a) Responsibilities of Partners and Supervisory Lawyers..............7
        (1) Measures of Complying with Rules...................................7

        (a) Scope of Application...7
        (2) Lawyer with Direct Supervisory Authority 7
        (3) Supervisory Lawyer's Responsibility for Another Lawyer's Violation......7
    b) Responsibilities Regarding Non-Lawyer Assistants.......................8
    c) Responsibilities of a Subordinate Lawyer 8
    d) Professional Independence of a Lawyer 8
        (1) Forming Partnership with Non-Lawyer 8
        (2) Lawyer's Professional Judgment 8
        (3) Involvement of Non-Lawyer..9
  J. Restrictions on Right to Practice 9
    1) <u>RESTRICTIONS ON RIGHT TO PRACTICE</u>............................9
    a) Employment or Other Relationship 9
    b) Settlement of a Client Controversy 9
  Review Questions 10

II. THE CLIENT-LAWYER RELATIONSHIP....................................16
  A. Formation of Client-Lawyer Relationship...............................16
    1) <u>MUTUAL AGREEMENT</u>..16
    a) Accepting Appointments 16
    b) Detrimental Reliance 16
        (1) Example 16
    2) <u>ETHICAL CONSIDERATIONS FOR ACCEPTING CLIENTS</u> ...17
  B. Scope, Objective and Means of the Representation....................17
    1) <u>SCOPE OF REPRESENTATION AND ALLOCATION OF AUTHORITY</u>.......17
    a) General Considerations..17
        (1) Client Decides Objectives of Representation 17
        (2) Lawyer Decides Means for Objectives......................................18
        (3) Lawyer Has Implied Authority to Act for Client.......................18
    b) Client with Diminished Capacity..18
  C. Decision-Making Authority – Actual and Apparent 18
    1) <u>ALLOCATION OF AUTHORITY</u> 18
    a) Authority Always Reserved to Client..19
    b) Authority Always Reserved to Lawyer...19
    2) <u>WHEN LAWYER HAS ACTUAL OR APPARENT AUTHORITY</u>...........19
    a) Lawyer's Actual Authority 19
    b) Lawyer's Apparent Authority 19
  D. Counsel and Assistance Within the Bounds of the Law 19
  E. Termination of the Client-Lawyer Relationship........................19
    1) <u>DECLINING OR TERMINATING REPRESENTATION</u>.............19
    a) Discharge by Lawyer – Mandatory Withdrawal............................20
    b) Discharge by Lawyer – Permissive Withdrawal...........................20
        (1) Obligation to Tribunal..20
    2) <u>DISCHARGE BY CLIENT</u>...20
    3) <u>DUTIES UPON DISCHARGE</u>...21
  F. Client-Lawyer Contracts...21
    1) <u>GENERAL RULE</u> 21

        a) Exception for Subsequent Formation or Modification 21
        b) Exception for Post-Representation Formation..21
        c) Interpretation of Contract – Reasonable Person Standard 21
     2) AGREEMENTS LIMITING CLIENT OR LAWYER DUTIES 22
        a) Lawyer and Client Can Limit Lawyer's Duties.....................................22
        b) Lawyer Can Waive Client's Duties 22
  G. Communications with Client 22
     1) DUTY TO INFORM AND CONSULT WITH CLIENT...............................22
  H. Fees...22
     1) FEE AGREEMENTS..22
        a) General Principles..23
        b) Reasonable Fee Requirement...23
        c) Communications Regarding Fees 23
     2) CONTINGENCY FEES 23
        a) Prohibited for Criminal and Domestic Matters.....................................23
        b) Contingency Fee Agreements 24
     3) FEE SPLITTING WITH OTHER LAWYERS 24
  I.   Sale of Law Practice...24
  Review Questions 26

III. CLIENT CONFIDENTIALITY 33
  A. Attorney-Client Privilege 33
     1) WHEN STATE LAW OF EVIDENTIARY PRIVILEGES APPLIES 33
     2) GENERAL LAW OF EVIDENTIARY PRIVILEGES.................................33
        a) Privileged Communications...33
        b) Holder of the Privilege..33
        c) General Exceptions to the Privilege...34
           (1) Examples..34
  B. Work Product Doctrine...34
  C. Professional Obligation of Confidentiality 34
     1) DUTIES TO PROSPECTIVE CLIENT 35
     2) CONFIDENTIALITY OF INFORMATION 35
  D. Disclosures Expressly or Impliedly Authorized by Client 35
     1) CLIENT-AUTHORIZED DISCLOSURE..35
        a) Express Consent...35
        b) Implied Consent...35
  E. Other Exceptions to the Confidentiality Rule 36
  Review Questions 37

IV. CONFLICTS OF INTEREST 40
  A. Current Client Conflicts – Multiple Clients and Joint Representation 40
     1) MULTIPLE CLIENTS 40
        a) General Rule – Client 1 v. Client 2..40
           (1) Exceptions..40
     2) JOINT REPRESENTATION 40
        a) Aggregate Settlement...40

B. Current Client Conflicts – Lawyer's Personal Interest or Duties..................41
C. Former Client Conflicts..41
  1) DUTIES TO FORMER CLIENTS 41
    a) General Rule – Client v. Former Client 41
    b) Former Firm 41
    c) Use of Former Client's Information 41
    d) Former and Current Government Officers and Employees 41
D. Prospective Client Conflicts...42
E. Imputed Conflicts..42
  1) LAWYERS ASSOCIATED IN A FIRM 42
    a) Exceptions..42
      (1) No Significant Risk of Limiting Representation 43
      (2) Screening..43
  2) LAWYER DISSOCIATED FROM A FIRM 43
  3) WAIVER 43
F. Acquiring an Interest in Litigation 43
G. Business Transactions with Client...44
  1) LIMITATIONS ON BUSINESS TRANSACTIONS WITH CLIENT 44
  2) USE OF CLIENT'S INFORMATION 44
  3) LIMITATION ON GIFTS 44
  4) MEDIA OR LITERARY RIGHTS 44
  5) FINANCIAL ASSISTANCE TO CLIENT 44
  6) SEXUAL RELATIONS WITH CLIENT 45
H. Third-Party Compensation and Influence..45
I. Lawyers Currently or Formerly in Government Service 45
J. Former Judge, Arbitrator, Mediator, or Other Third-Party Neutral.........45
Review Questions 47

V. COMPETENCE, MALPRACTICE, AND OTHER CIVIL LIABILITY 52
A. Maintaining Competence 52
  1) DUTY OF COMPETENCE..52
  2) OBLIGATION TO MAINTAIN COMPETENCE 52
B. Competence Necessary to Undertake Representation...............................52
  1) COMPETENCE REQUIREMENT 52
  2) GAINING COMPETENCE..52
    a) Emergency Situations...53
C. Exercise of Diligence and Care 53
D. Civil Liability to Client Including Malpractice...53
  1) GENERAL CONSIDERATIONS 53
    a) Enforcement Proceedings 53
    b) Civil Liability...53
      (1) Legal Malpractice 54
E. Civil Liability to Non-Clients..54
  1) GENERAL DUTY..54
  2) SPECIFIC DUTY 54
F. Limiting Liability for Malpractice 55

    G. Malpractice Insurance and Risk Prevention..**55**
        1) <u>INSURANCE POLICY MAY PROTECT LAWYER FROM LIABILITY</u>...55
            a) Common Aspects of Insurance Policy...55
        2) <u>RISK PREVENTION SEEKS TO DECREASE LIABILITY EXPOSURE</u>...56
    Review Questions **57**

VI. LITIGATION AND OTHER FORMS OF ADVOCACY **60**
    A. Meritorious Claims and Contentions..**60**
        1) <u>LAWYER CANNOT BRING FRIVOLOUS CLAIM</u> 60
        2) <u>FEDERAL RULE OF CIVIL PROCEDURE 11</u>.......................................60
            a) Signature Requirement...60
            b) Representations...60
                (1) No Improper Purpose 60
                (2) Legal Grounding 60
                (3) Evidentiary Support 60
                (4) Denials 61
            c) Process for Sanctions 61
                (1) By Motion 61
                      (a) Opportunity to Correct...61
                      (b) Expenses and Fees Available...61
                (2) On Court's Initiative 61
            d) Nature of Sanctions 61
    B. Expediting Litigation **62**
    C. Candor to the Tribunal **62**
        1) <u>FALSE REPRESENTATIONS ARE PROHIBITED</u> 62
            a) False Statements...62
            b) Binding Legal Authority 62
            c) False Evidence 62
         2) <u>LAWYER'S SUBSEQUENT REMEDIAL MEASURES</u> 62
            a) Duration of Duties...63
         3) <u>DISCLOSURE OF MATERIAL FACTS IN *EX-PARTE* PROCEEDINGS</u>...63
    D. Fairness to Opposing Party and Counsel **63**
        1) <u>EVIDENCE</u>...63
            a) Access to Evidence 63
            b) Falsification of Evidence 63
            c) Discovery Requests...63
            d) Request to Not Disclose Relevant Information 63
        2) <u>TRIAL</u>...63
         3) <u>DISOBEY RULES OF TRIBUNAL</u> 64
         4) <u>THREATS</u>..64
            a) Criminal Charges 64
            b) Disciplinary Charges..64
    E. Impartiality and Decorum of the Tribunal **64**
        1) <u>IMPROPER CONTACT WITH COURT AND JURORS</u> 64
    F. Trial Publicity..**64**
        1) <u>NO PREJUDICIAL EXTRAJUDICIAL STATEMENTS</u> 64

      a) Exception for Responsive Statement 65
  G. Lawyer as Witness **65**
  Review Questions **66**

VII. COMMUNICATIONS WITH PERSONS OTHER THAN CLIENTS 71
  A. Truthfulness in Statements to Others **71**
    1) <u>NO FALSE STATEMENTS OF FACT</u> 71
    2) <u>NO FAILURE TO DISCLOSE MATERIAL FACT ASSISTING CRIME</u> ...71
    3) <u>DISTINGUISHING STATEMENTS MADE DURING NEGOTIATIONS</u>......71
  B. Communication with Represented Persons **71**
  C. Communications with Unrepresented Persons **71**
  D. Respect for Rights of Third Parties **72**
    1) <u>HARASSING OTHERS</u> 72
    2) <u>INADVERTENT DISCLOSURE OF INFORMATION</u> 72
  Review Questions **73**

VIII. DIFFERENT ROLES OF THE LAWYER **75**
  A. Lawyer as Advisor **75**
  B. Lawyer as Evaluator **75**
    1) <u>EVALUATION FOR USE BY THIRD PERSONS</u> 75
  C. Lawyer as Negotiator **75**
  D. Lawyer as Arbitrator, Mediator, or Other Third-Party Neutral **75**
  E. Prosecutors and Other Governmental Lawyers **76**
    1) <u>SPECIAL RESPONSIBILITIES OF PROSECUTORS DURING CASE</u> 76
    2) <u>DUTY OF PROSECUTOR TO DISCLOSE INFORMATION</u>
       <u>CONCERNING CONVICTION</u> 76
       a) New Credible and Material Evidence 76
       b) Clear and Convincing Evidence...77
    3) <u>DUTY OF PROSECUTOR TO REFRAIN FROM MAKING</u>
       <u>EXTRAJUDICIAL COMMENTS</u>...77
  F. Lawyer Appearing in Non-Adjudicative Proceeding **77**
  G. Lawyer Representing an Entity or Other Organization **77**
    1) <u>GENERAL DUTY TO ORGANIZATION</u> 77
    2) <u>VIOLATIONS OF LEGAL OBLIGATIONS OR LAWS</u> 77
    3) <u>ADVERSE ORGANIZATION AND CONSTITUENTS</u> 78
    4) <u>DUAL REPRESENTATION</u>...78
  Review Questions **79**

IX. SAFEKEEPING FUNDS AND OTHER PROPERTY **82**
  A. Establishing and Maintaining Client Trust Accounts **82**
    1) <u>CLIENT TRUST ACCOUNTS</u> 82
       a) Account Located in State of Office 82
       b) Complete Records Must be Kept for Five Years 82
       c) Limited Exception for Paying Bank Service Charges 82
  B. Safekeeping Funds and Other Property of Clients **82**
    1) <u>SEPARATION OF PROPERTY</u> 82

    C. Safekeeping Funds and Other Property of Third Persons............................**82**
    D. Disputed Claims **83**
        1) TYPES OF DISPUTES...83
        2) CONTROL OF FUNDS 83
            a) Funds Must Be Separate 83
            b) Undisputed Funds Must Be Promptly Returned 83
            c) Lawyer can Withhold Funds for Fees if Risk Exists 83
            d) Dispute Between Client and Third Party 83
    Review Questions **85**

X. COMMUNICATION ABOUT LEGAL SERVICES **87**
    A. Advertising and Other Public Communications About Legal Services..........**87**
        1) COMMUNICATION CONCERNING A LAWYER'S SERVICES 87
            a) Must Be Truthful...87
            b) Unjustified Expectations 87
            c) Unfair Comparisons 87
        2) ADVERTISING..87
            a) Contents of Advertisements 87
            b) Keeping Copies of Advertisements 87
            c) Place of Advertisements 87
        3) FIRM NAMES AND LETTERHEAD 88
            a) Not False or Misleading...88
            b) Partner Serving in Public Office 88
            c) Representation as Partnership 88
            d) Jurisdiction Admissions 88
    B. Solicitation - Direct Contact with Prospective Clients **88**
        1) REAL-TIME SOLICITATION PROHIBITED 88
            a) Exception to Prohibition 88
        2) OTHER SOLICITATION PERMISSIBLE 89
            a) Exception to Allowable Solicitations...89
            b) "Advertising Material"...89
        3) SOLICITATION BY THIRD PARTIES 89
    C. Group Legal Services...**89**
    D. Referrals...**89**
        1) PAYMENT FOR RECOMMENDING A LAWYER'S SERVICES 89
            a) Reasonable Costs of Advertisements or Communications 90
            b) Legal Service Plans and Certain Lawyer Referral Services 90
            c) Purchase of Law Practice..90
            d) Reciprocal Referral Agreement 90
    E. Communication of Fields of Practice and Specialization................................**90**
        1) FIELDS OF PRACTICE 90
            a) Patent Lawyers...90
            b) Admiralty Lawyers 90
        2) SPECIALIZATION 90
    Review Questions **92**

XI. LAWYERS' DUTIES TO THE PUBLIC AND THE LEGAL SYSTEM............**95**
    A. Voluntary *Pro Bono* Service..**95**
        1) <u>SUBSTANTIAL MAJORITY OF SERVICES</u>...........................95
        2) <u>FOCUS OF VOLUNTARY SERVICE</u>...................................95
    B. Accepting Appointments...**95**
    C. Serving in Legal Services Organizations...**95**
    D. Law Reform Activities Affecting Client Interests..........................**96**
    E. Criticism of Judges and Adjudicating Officials..............................**96**
    F. Political Contributions to Obtain Engagements or Appointments.......**96**
        1) <u>POLITICAL CONTRIBUTION</u>...96
        2) <u>GOVERNMENT LEGAL ENGAGEMENT/JUDICIAL APPOINTMENT</u>.......96
    G. Improper Influence on Government Official....................................**97**
    H. Assisting Judicial Misconduct..**97**
    I. Impropriety Incident to Public Service...**97**
        1) <u>LAWYERS AS JUDICIAL CANDIDATES</u>............................97
    Review Questions...**98**

XII. JUDICIAL CONDUCT..**100**
    A. Maintaining the Independence and Impartiality of the Judiciary........**100**
        1) <u>COMPLIANCE WITH THE LAW</u>....................................100
        2) <u>PROMOTING CONFIDENCE IN THE JUDICIARY</u>..............100
            a) Independence, Integrity, and Impartiality Defined....................100
            b) Avoiding Impropriety and the Appearance of Impropriety.....................100
                (1) Test for Appearance of Impropriety......................101
        3) <u>AVOIDING ABUSE OF THE PRESTIGE OF JUDICIAL OFFICE</u>.......101
            a) Improper Use of Judicial Office..............................101
    B. Performing the Duties of Judicial Office Impartially,
    Competently, and Diligently..**101**
        1) <u>GIVING PRECEDENCE TO THE DUTIES OF JUDICIAL OFFICE</u>.......101
        2) <u>IMPARTIALITY AND FAIRNESS</u>..................................101
        3) <u>BIAS, PREJUDICE, AND HARASSMENT</u>.......................102
            a) Judges Must Perform Judicial Duties without Bias or Prejudice.......102
            b) Judges May Not Manifest Bias or Prejudice, or Harassment..............102
            c) Judges Must Require Lawyers to Refrain from Improper Conduct.......102
        4) <u>EXTERNAL INFLUENCES ON JUDICIAL CONDUCT</u>...........102
            a) Public Clamor or Fear of Criticism May Not Sway Judges.................102
            b) Certain Relationships or Interests May Not Influence Judges.............102
            c) No Conveying that One Occupies Position to Influence Judges.........103
        5) <u>COMPETENCE, DILIGENCE, AND COOPERATION</u>..........103
            a) Requirements of Competence and Diligence...........................103
            b) Requirement of Cooperation..103
        6) <u>ENSURING THE RIGHT TO BE HEARD</u>.........................103
            a) Judge Must Provide the Right to Be Heard.............................103
            b) Judge May Encourage Settlement of Disputed Matters.................103
        7) <u>RESPONSIBILITY TO DECIDE</u>....................................104
        8) <u>DECORUM, DEMEANOR, AND COMMUNICATIONS WITH JURORS</u>...104

9) JUDICIAL STATEMENTS ON IMPENDING AND PENDING CASES...104
    a) Definition of Impending Matter and Pending Matter 104
    b) Judge May Not Make Certain Types of Statements 104
        (1) Judge Must Require Others to Refrain from Statements 104
        (2) Certain Exceptions Exist..105
        (3) Judge May Respond to Certain Types of Allegations 105
    c) What Judge May Not Say Regarding Anticipated Matters..........105
10) SUPERVISORY DUTIES 105
    a) Court Staff, Court Officials, and Others 105
    b) Judge with Supervisory Authority 105
11) ADMINISTRATIVE APPOINTMENTS.......................................105
    a) General Limitations on Judge's Power of Appointment..........105
    b) Election Contribution Limit on Judge's Power of Appointment.....106
        (1) Exceptions to Limits on Judge's Appointments 106
    c) Judge May Not Approve Compensation Greater than Fair Value..........106
12) DISABILITY AND IMPAIRMENT 106
    a) When Judge Must Take Action about Impairment................106
        (1) What Constitutes Appropriate Action..........................106
13) RESPONDING TO JUDICIAL AND LAWYER MISCONDUCT.............106
    a) Another Judge's Code Violation.................................106
    b) A Lawyer's Rules Violation 107
14) COOPERATION WITH DISCIPLINARY AUTHORITIES......................107
    a) Requirement of Judge's Cooperation.............................107
    b) Prohibition of Judge's Retaliation 107
C. Ex Parte Communications 107
1) GENERALLY, NO EX PARTE COMMUNICATION BY JUDGE...........107
    a) Scope of General Prohibition on Ex Parte Communications.........107
    b) When Judge May Engage in Ex Parte Communications 108
        (1) Scheduling, Administrative, or Emergency Purposes............108
        (2) Disinterested Expert's Advice 108
        (3) Court Officials, Court Staff, and Other Judges................108
            (a) Limits on Consultation with Other Judges 108
        (4) Parties and Their Lawyers 109
        (5) Authorized by Law 109
2) INADVERTENT RECEIPT OF EX PARTE COMMUNICATION 109
3) CANNOT INVESTIGATE AND IS LIMITED TO EVIDENCE/FACTS ...109
4) ENSURE COMPLIANCE ABOUT EX PARTE COMMUNICATIONS 109
D. Disqualification 109
1) WHEN IMPARTIALITY MIGHT REASONABLY BE QUESTIONED....109
    a) Personal Bias or Prejudice 110
    b) Personal Knowledge 110
    c) Certain Types of Connections to Proceedings....................110
    d) Economic Interests...110
        (1) De Minimis Interest 110
    e) Contributions to Judge's Campaign.............................110
    f) Statement by Judge Regarding Issue 111

		g)	Judge Served as Lawyer	111
		h)	Judge was Associated with Lawyer	111
		i)	Judge Served in Governmental Employment	111
		j)	Judge Served as Material Witness	111
		k)	Judge Presided as Judge	111
	2)	JUDGE'S PERSONAL AND FIDUCIARY ECONOMIC INTERESTS		111
	3)	WAIVER OF DISQUALIFICATION		111
	4)	NECESSITY MAY OVERRIDE DISQUALIFICATION		112

E. Extrajudicial Activities..**112**

1) LIMITATIONS ON JUDGE'S EXTRAJUDICIAL ACTIVITIES 112
   a) Interfering with Proper Performance of Judicial Duties 112
   b) Leading to Frequent Disqualification 112
   c) Undermining Independence, Integrity, or Impartiality 112
      (1) Discriminatory Conduct; Expressions of Prejudice or Bias 113
   d) Appearing to be Coercive 113
   e) Using Court Resources 113
2) APPEARANCES BEFORE GOVERNMENTAL BODIES AND CONSULTATION WITH GOVERNMENT OFFICIALS 113
   a) Generally, No Appearances at Public Hearings or Consultation 113
3) APPOINTMENTS TO GOVERNMENTAL POSITIONS 113
4) TESTIFYING AS CHARACTER WITNESS 114
   a) Abuse of Prestige of Office by Testifying as Character Witness 114
5) USE OF NONPUBLIC INFORMATION 114
6) AFFILIATION WITH DISCRIMINATORY ORGANIZATIONS 114
   a) Prohibited Membership Gives Appearance of Impropriety 114
7) PARTICIPATION IN EDUCATIONAL, RELIGIOUS, CHARITABLE FRATERNAL, OR CIVIL ORGANIZATIONS AND ACTIVITIES 114
   a) Activities Sponsored by Organizations or Governmental Entities 115
   b) Activities of Non-Profit Organizations 115
   c) Judge Can Participate in Activities of Organizations or Entities............115
8) APPOINTMENTS TO FIDUCIARY POSITIONS..................................115
   a) Fiduciary for Family Member under Limited Circumstances 115
   b) When Judge May Not Serve as Fiduciary..116
9) SERVICE AS ARBITRATOR OR MEDIATOR 116
10) PRACTICE OF LAW 116
11) FINANCIAL, BUSINESS, OR REMUNERATIVE ACTIVITIES..............116
   a) Permitted Financial Activities...116
      (1) Holding and Managing Investments 116
      (2) Serving in Certain Capacities in Business Entities............................116
   b) When a Judge May Not Engage in Permitted Financial Activities 116
12) COMPENSATION FOR EXTRAJUDICIAL ACTIVITIES 117
13) ACCEPTANCE AND REPORTING OF GIFTS, LOANS, BEQUESTS, BENEFITS, OR OTHER THINGS OF VALUE...................................117
   a) When Judge Must Not Accept Something of Value...............................117
   b) When Judge May Accept Something of Value without Reporting It 117
      (1) Items with Little Intrinsic Value 117

        (2) Things from Those Whom Disqualification is Required 117
        (3) Ordinary Social Hospitality 118
        (4) Financial or Commercial Opportunities and Benefits 118
        (5) Prizes and Rewards Given in Public Contests 118
        (6) Fellowships, Scholarships, and Similar Items 118
        (7) Resource Materials Provided by Publishers 118
        (8) Awards, Gifts, or Benefits 118
   c) When Judge May Accept Things of Value with Reporting 118
        (1) Gifts Incident to Public Testimonial 118
        (2) Invitations for Free Attendance of Certain Events 118
        (3) Things of Value from Certain Types of Parties or Attorneys 119
14) REIMBURSEMENT OF EXPENSES, WAIVERS OF FEES/CHARGES .. 119
   a) General Considerations about Certain Reimbursement Waivers 119
   b) When Judge May Accept Certain Reimbursement Waivers 119
        (1) Limitation on Permissible Reimbursement 119
   c) Public Reporting Requirement 119
15) PUBLIC REPORTING REQUIREMENTS 119
   a) Public Documents 119
   b) Public Report Contents 120
   c) Timing of Public Report 120
   d) What Must Be Publicly Reported 120
Review Questions 121

BAR REVIEW COURSES

AmeriBar offers comprehensive bar review courses in over 30 jurisdictions. Complete courses start under $1000. Visit http://www.ameribar.com for more information. Visit http://www.ameribar.com/videos for hundreds of video and written testimonials.

Testimonials

"AmeriBar provided me with all the tools needed to pass the bar. While studying, I had a lot of questions and concerns. AmeriBar staff was always available and provided me with honest and detailed feedback so that I could understand what I was doing wrong. I would recommend AmeriBar over other bar courses not only because of the great value of the course, but also because the books and audio lectures provided me all of the information I needed to learn to pass."

" I just wanted to let you know that I PASSED THE ILLINOIS BAR EXAM!!! :) Yay!!! I wanted to say "thank you" so much for your wonderful bar course and great people like you who have always been supportive and nice. This is more than just a bar review course - it's a phenomenal support system, too! AmeriBar has changed my life for the better!!!!!!! I have attached my pass letter which I got today. Thank you, thank you, thank you!!! I saw the recommendations on your website from people who've used AmeriBar and, if I can give a recommendation for your company to others, please let me know. I would be more than happy to do so. All of my friends and family know about AmeriBar already and how great it is! :) Thank you again and I hope that you and everyone at AmeriBar have a fantastic day!!!! Y'all ROCK!!!! :)"

"It gives me great pleasure to announce that I have passed the July West Virginia Bar Exam. I cannot thank you enough for your professionalism and encouragement. With your guidance I was able to increase my MEE score by a remarkable *32* *points*! I didn't just pass the bar, I demolished it. I hope future students of the program have similar results, and I wish you and AmeriBar continued success. Forever grateful, SG, Tutoring Student."

"I completed the AmeriBar tutoring program in advance of the February exam here in Minnesota, and wanted to email you with my sincerest thanks for connecting me with my tutor. With her help, I honed my essay writing skills to such a degree that I confidently sat for the exam and PASSED. I was a re-taker, so I'm particularly thrilled to have this part of my legal career in the rear view mirror. Please know that I will not hesitate to recommend AmeriBar to those who might be considering a Bar prep course. Again, many thanks for offering a wonderful preparation product."

"If you are a repeat taker or you have not taken the test in some time, i.e. 5-7 years, I highly recommend [tutoring]. The tutoring program allows for one-on-one interaction and is absolutely essential if you are not a self-motivator. Being responsible for assignments and clear meeting times was crucial to my success. I am just grateful that I finally found a service that was focused on my success and not just turning out a product that is produced for the masses. . . . I learned much more of the law using AmeriBar then I ever did with [a competing course]...."

"I found the introductory lectures helpful in helping me understand why AmeriBar is different from other courses. . . . AmeriBar is the program to choose for a personalized study program that helps identify each student's specific needs, weaknesses, and strengths. The tutors are knowledgeable, experienced, and provide helpful feedback. Neither of these aspects is offered by some of the other major "name brand" courses. Additionally, I had been told repeatedly by other courses and professors that home-study courses are not recommended and that that's probably why I had failed previously. I refused to accept this answer. I lived an hour and a half from either of the courses offered here in CO and found that the commute was an incredible waste of time - not to mention that I would have to put my child in daycare just for the Bar exam course. AmeriBar is used to working with student[s] by long distance and made the home study course work for me - THANK YOU!"

"It looks like all the tutoring worked out for me and I will sing the praises of the program to any who will listen."

"AmeriBar outlines were straight to the point. Other bar prep programs bog you down in superfluous information and make you feel overwhelmed. AmeriBar simplifies it and lets you know what areas are tested more than others on the bar. I was most impressed by the one on one tutoring I got. It really made me analyze how I was writing my essays and choosing my MBE answers. Other bar preps don't do this. I already have told a friend about this and she has signed up! The one on one tutoring makes a HUGE difference. The outlines and substantive law is taught very clearly without confusing the issues. It taught me how to study more proficiently and effectively in order to pass the bar. My scores substantially increased after this program, particularly my essay portion. AmeriBar is great and I would recommend it to anyone! . . ."

"Thank you so much for all of your help! I passed the bar exam!!! I wanted to let you know that all of the last minute MPT prep really paid off. I scored a perfect score on one of the MPTs and a 5 on the other. I think that greatly helped me score out in the end because they were worth so much! Thanks again!!!!!"

"Life has been hectic, but I wanted to let AmeriBar know that I passed the bar on my fifth attempt. I went up 13 points on my MBE score and 10 points on my MEE/MPT score. We need a 270 to pass in West Virginia and I got 280! AmeriBar really helped! There were concepts that I had never seen before in using [a competing course] the four previous times. AmeriBar gave me what I need to actually achieve my dream of becoming an attorney!"

"When you want to join the crowd, take another course, when you have to pass the bar, take AmeriBar."

"[AmeriBar] offered a more comprehensive program available for a student to get started early - ahead of [competition] and for less money."

"I had used [a competitor] before and was unsuccessful so I was looking for something new. I came across your website and the price as well as the ability to buy things a la carte was appealing. . . Definitely would recommend it over the other options. The pages were not cluttered up with diagrams and charts but strictly stuck to the law. The study schedule was very helpful since I was studying on my own. Customer service was great in that I didn't need to use it since everything arrived on time and in good condition. This was the 5th time I took the test (1st in Connecticut) and AmeriBar finally got me through it! . . . [A]fter 4 tries it was thanks to AmeriBar that I will soon have Esq after my name!!"

"The cost! Such a savings! . . . [I]t is a great choice for people who want to save money and don't need the rigorous structure of other bar review programs. It is a fraction of the cost but just as effective."

"First and foremost, I loved the program. . . . I thought the lectures were thorough and complete. . . . I thought the value of your program was right on. [I]t is ridiculous to follow [a competitor's] schedule when there are areas you don't know as well. I mean, two days total on Property? Give me a break. I took nearly a week to learn all of property (and there was an essay and the 34 MBE questions, so it was time well spent.) The flexibility of your program, and the ease of going back over things and hearing them again was great, and I told friends of it. Also, I thought the essay book was, as the kids say, the bomb. I had some loose leaf pages of old essays that someone handed off to me, and I shiver to think I thought those would be enough. I did a dozen evidence essays by test day, with great summary answers. . . . Again, I really liked the program, and I was particularly thankful to receive the Oregon essay book AFTER I had paid for no additional cost! That was so so generous of you. Thank you. I rocked the essays on test day, and I know it was because I had simply done so many of them from your book. . . . Have I said I loved our program? Because I did. . . . I really thank you for all your support. The materials were very helpful and I am glad I found you. I used my savings from [not using a competitor's course] on an airline ticket to Australia after the Bar where I drank cold beer and shrimp off the barbi."

"I just want you to know that I really did appreciate the AmeriBar system and I can't say enough about it. Those MBE questions, in my opinion, were one of the most useful parts of the whole system. I tell everyone that AmeriBar is the way to go!"

"It's just great. From the service to the insight of how to approach the exam everything worked beautifully. I am from Puerto Rico and I passed the Oregon Bar without even going to law school in Oregon. All I knew about Oregon law was what AmeriBar provided."

"AmeriBar, by far, had the best deal for the money. The amount of materials and the quality of those materials could not be equaled. AmeriBar had a great reputation for quality and customer service according to my pre-bar research. Plus, you cannot beat having the hundreds and hundreds of practice MBE questions accessible to you. The outlines were fantastic and allowed me to focus my studying on areas where I had the most trouble. They were clear, concise, and well written. I used them almost to the exclusion of all other materials for the first month."

"Anyone can compile a bunch of rules under headings and sub-headings. It takes unique care to blend an outline format and well-written prose. That's what AmeriBar has done. ... [W]ith this kind of solid writing, students should be aware that a relaxed reading session can prove more valuable than a tedious day of note-taking."

"The AmeriBar program is lean and no-nonsense. It recognizes that the bar exam is a minimum-competence general-knowledge exam and focuses on getting students firmly into the passing zone rather than unrealistically focusing in on minutiae and perfectionism. Thanks to AmeriBar, I was able to actually keep on having a life while studying for the bar. Not only did this preserve my sanity -- I'm convinced it also helped me do better on the bar, since I went into the bar without having ground myself down to nubbins with stress. I was able to study at my own pace and keep focused on what was important in passing."

A friend recommended it to me and the price was much more affordable than other courses on the market. The outlines and lectures provided by AmeriBar were great. They contained the information that was current and relevant to pass the bar exam. I like the fact that I could choose what to study and when. I was very impressed by the accessibility of the AmeriBar staff. I was amazed when I called and a person actually answered the phone and I actually received response emails. The access to the staff made me feel that AmeriBar wanted me to pass and not just my money! I would definitely advise a friend to use AmeriBar. It is a great affordable program and the fact that you can study at your own pace is wonderful.
The fact that there are actually people to talk to and that you can go at your own pace.
I cannot stress the importance of the essay critiques and the email and phone access to AmeriBar. It was like having a personal tutor. I think the program was very pleasurable, if studying for the bar can be pleasurable!"

"I liked how concise the outlines were. I felt they hit on the important points. I LOVED the outlines for the multistate part. I would highly recommend the program, particularly if they have all ready [sic] passed one bar and are looking to take another state's bar, like me.
It's concise and doesn't have too much extra info in the outlines like other bar review courses."

"I would and have advised friends to use AmeriBar because the flexibility of the program is unmatched.... I am completely satisfied with every aspect of my experience."

"Your bar prep program is the best on the market. It's not even close. The lectures were short and to the point..No fluff...When you want to join the crowd, take another course, when you have to pass the bar, take AmeriBar. I was a repeat taker and I can give that insight. I worked less hours and passed. I took [a competitor's course] the first time and felt buried in practice problems and workload and overwhelmed. AmeriBar is streamlined and was easy to follow and I passed on the first try using AmeriBar. Don't consider it. Do it."

"I just got my bar exam results back and I wanted to first thank you and AmeriBar for your help in my passing the bar! In Michigan, a passing score is 135 out of 200, and I got a score of 168 (173/200 on the MBE and 164/200 on the Michigan essays). I'm really glad to have passed, and am grateful to everyone at AmeriBar for your assistance. I really liked AmeriBar's study program both because it prepared me well for the bar exam and because it allowed me to maximize the value of my study time. Unlike my friends that used another program, I felt exceptionally well-prepared for the MBE section of the bar exam. In addition, AmeriBar's study materials are tailored to the material most likely to be on the bar exam. This meant that I didn't waste time studying information that wasn't on the exam and also was able to more fully master the material that was on the exam. And when I had substantive questions about the study material, AmeriBar tutors were available by phone and email to help clear up my confusion. AmeriBar made my bar study so much less stressful and more rewarding, and I am so grateful for your help in passing the bar. Thank you!"

"I just wanted to write and let you know that I passed the bar, thanks in LARGE part to you!! I couldn't have done it without your help. I will recommend that everyone who asks comes directly to you all!"

"I chose AmeriBar because it is a thorough bar review course that allowed me the flexibility to study around my own schedule. . . . It's probably the best option for studying for the Bar. High quality materials, pointed questions and flexibility. All of my interactions with the staff were positive. I always received a quick reply."

"I just wanted to share with you good news that I was able to pass the bar this time. Needless to say, you helped me so much this past winter and I would not be able to make it without all the skills and advice you taught me. I know I asked you lots of questions... Thank you for your patience and time. Again, THANK YOU!"

"I am writing to tell you that I finally passed my bar exam.... I credit your methods for my success. I believe that if I would have outlined to learn at the beginning, I would have been successful earlier..........Thanks for everything... The tips that you gave me I wish I would have known in law school. Also my sister passed last year's bar. She raised her MBE by 17 points after using your outline."

"I just wanted to share the good news with you that I PASSED THE INDIANA BAR EXAMINATION!!! I want to thank you for all the hard work we did together and being such a great coach and mentor. Your strategies for the essays really helped me this time around, and I definitely had a different approach to the exam this time than I did the first time with Illinois.

Thank you so much for being such a good teacher, and to be honest the practice essays we did together were the essays that sort of reappeared on the bar exam this time!! I definitely want to share with AmeriBar my testament to how good of a service you all are!! Many thanks to you....will definitely work with you again when I redo Illinois bar!"

"I just want to let you know that I passed the Virginia Bar Exam! Thank you very much for all your help. My sessions with you gave me a lot of confidence going into the exam and helped me stay focused while I was taking the test."

"Your program explains the rules of law better …. than quick black letter statements of the law which I saw in [a competing course's] outlines. By narrowing in on the basic principles, and giving a better historical foundation, I felt that I was able to remember and understand areas of the law that I did not take in law school."

"Your program was a success for me. I was working full-time clerking for a judge while I studied for the bar and I was able to do it with your program. I failed the bar when I had all the time in the world taking [a competing course]. I felt that your program was more focused and accessible."

"I felt the essay lectures were superb. . . . . I was focused on every word he said and took scrupulous notes. I would tell [a friend considering AmeriBar] that they'd be a darn fool to not go with AmeriBar! AmeriBar (to my knowledge) is the only bar review course that offers actual RELEASED MBE QUESTIONS from the NCBE AND STATE SPECIFIC ESSAY questions and answers! What better way to get into the minds of the examiners?"

"I passed CT on my first try after many failed attempts at NY. I tried [MBE specialist course competitor] (3 times!), [national seminar based course competitor] (twice!), [essay writing specialist competitor] (a Harvard Essay "expert"), [online bar review competitor] (horrendous waste of money and time), and I can go on and on and on... As stated before, the fact that the questions offered by AmeriBar are RELEASED coupled with the process . . . really helped me to learn the law. Also, the lecturer insisted that the candidate not focus on quantity when doing MBE questions (unlike [competitor]), but to focus on the quality of learning the nuances."

"Your program focuses on the important and frequently-tested subjects, and is realistic, whereas other programs are overly and unnecessarily comprehensive. Your program worked really well for me. It emphasized the right subjects and strategies, and I think it works really well for repeat takers such as myself."

"I just wanted to personally thank you for your unbelievably effective bar review course and to let you know I passed the July District of Columbia Bar Exam! My story is a bit different than most though, so I wanted to share it with you. You see, I graduated from law school in 1983; yes, 26 years ago. During that period, for reasons I won't go into as it's kind of a long story, I had never taken the bar exam in any jurisdiction. Also, I had never worked in any law-related

field at any time during those 26 years. However, I decided that after all these years, it was time to change that and challenge the exam. I enrolled in your complete District of Columbia course including the essay writing and feedback portion (not the tutoring), as well as the MPRE review. I followed your instructions, listened to the online lectures, and completed the practice essays. Now, after 26 years of not being involved with the law at all, and only using your course to prepare, I can say I'm a lawyer! Words cannot express my heartfelt gratitude to the folks at Ameribar who have made this long-delayed dream come true for me. In case you are wondering, although I don't know what my MEE and MPT scores were, my MBE score was 146.2 and the MPRE score was 87. Thank you again for your fantastic course. [I]t's simply amazing."

"It[']s been a hectic last few weeks, but I wanted to tell you that I passed the Oregon State bar exam. It's such a relief. Thanks so much for keeping me on track with writing those essays and MPTs, even though I was flustered most of the time while we were talking. I felt very comfortable during the exam and even felt like I wrote a very good persuasive MPT."

"I used your company's materials exclusively for the July Michigan bar and wanted to happily report that I passed, and comfortably. I'm proud that I did so well, while spending a third of what many of my cohorts spent on review materials and questions. I didn't even get to a lot of your MBE questions, and I still got a 156! The big review companies are running a racket, scaring students into thinking they need to spend $3K to pass the bar, and I'm glad a company is out there offering an alternative."

"I passed the Ohio bar exam in the 91st percentile. I took the exam ten years after graduating from law school, while working full-time and raising five children. The only study materials I bought and used were from Ameribar. You got me where I need to be. Thanks."

"I thought AmeriBar really handled the MBE well. The outlines were excellent and I enjoyed the online question bank."

"The majority of students go with [a competing course] not because [the competing course] is the superior way of studying for the bar, but because everyone else is doing it. For people who don't mind breaking from the herd Ameribar is a great way of preparing for the bar. Everything you need to pass the bar exam is provided."

"Get it. It works. . . . I liked the multiple suggested study schedules depending upon the amount of time a candidate has to study -- very helpful."

"I preferred the flexibility of studying on my own time vs attending scheduled classroom lectures. I thought the outlines were really good. . . . I thought the lectures on IRAC and exam writing were really good. . . . I thought AmeriBar really handled the MBE well. The outlines were excellent and I enjoyed the online question bank. In addition to AmeriBar, I also had the [COMPETITOR'S] 6 day foundation course. Although [COMPETITOR] specializes in the

MBE, I greatly preferred AmeriBar's materials to prepare for the MBE. . . Many law students have a "herd" mentality. The majority of students go with [COMPETITOR] not because [COMPETITOR] is the superior way of studying for the bar, but because everyone else is doing it. For people who don't mind breaking from the herd Ameribar is a great way of preparing for the bar. Everything you need to pass the bar exam is provided. The flexibility of the program makes Ameribar different. I tried to follow the study calendar provided, but I knew that some subjects came easier to me than others and I had the flexibility to spend extra time on subjects which I found more difficult. . . ."

"The written and other materials TELLING us how to approach studying really kept me on track . . . very very very helpful stuff. I followed it pretty closely. VERY good program, approach, lectures, written materials, all excellent. . . . And, of course, I'm thrilled I passed!!!!! Thanks for your help. . . . I am a 27 year Colorado lawyer and found your "system" worked very well for all kinds of reasons and probably for all kinds of "students" and their learning styles. . . . As I said above, I was impressed, very much so, with your system, and I bet it[']s helped a lot of law students pass the bar exam."

"I wanted to send a huge thank you today because I just found out I passed the bar exam!!!! I know it was due to your efforts in helping me prepare and create a more concise essay and I appreciate all the tips you gave me to approach the MBE. I scored a 142 on the essays and a 152 on the MBE. Georgia requires a 270 to pass so I even had some points to spare. :) I can't believe I went from a 246 to a 294 (and they even tested us with a tricky Secured Transactions question)! There truly are no words to describe the joy I'm feeling right now. Thank you from the bottom of my heart."

"I was just writing to let you know that I passed the Bar Exam this time around. I improved a little bit on the MBE but on the essays I improved by almost 20 points which was my saving grace this time. I owe it all to you and the feedback you provided on the numerous essays that I wrote and you critiqued. It seemed so much easier writing the essays this time around. I really appreciate all the work and time you put into helping me succeed on the exam."

MPRE BASICS

General Considerations

This Professional Responsibility outline covers material that has traditionally been tested on the Multistate Professional Responsibility Exam (MPRE). The MPRE is drafted by the National Conference of Bar Examiners (NCBE). It consists of 60 multiple choice questions. You will also be asked to complete 10 Test Center Review questions regarding your impressions of the testing conditions. The exam lasts two hours and five minutes.

The American Bar Association (ABA) has promulgated Model Rules of Professional Conduct, which are referred to herein as the "Rule(s)" and cited as the "Model Rules of Prof'l Conduct R. ___." Almost all states have adopted the Rules. The Rules are heavily tested on the MPRE. Accordingly, it is important to learn, know, and understand them.

The MPRE will also test legal principles other than those found in the Rules. The MPRE tests legal principles found in the ABA's Model Code of Judicial Conduct, which is referred to herein as the "Code" and cited as the "Model Code of Judicial Conduct." Another source of testable legal principles is the American Law Institute's *Restatement of the Law, 3d—Law Governing Lawyers*. It is referred to herein as the "Restatement" and cited as the "Restatement of the Law Governing Lawyers, Third, § ___." Finally, according to the National Conference of Bar Examiners (NCBE)

> [The MPRE also tests] controlling constitutional decisions and generally accepted principles established in leading federal and state cases and in procedural and evidentiary rules. The remaining items, outside the disciplinary context, are designed to measure an understanding of the generally accepted rules, principles, and common law regulating the legal profession in the United States; in these items, the correct answer will be governed by the view reflected in a majority of cases, statutes, or regulations on the subject. To the extent that questions of professional responsibility arise in the context of procedural or evidentiary issues, such as the availability of litigation sanctions or the scope of the attorney-client evidentiary privilege, the Federal Rules of Civil Procedure and the Federal Rules of Evidence will be assumed to apply, unless otherwise stated.

Some of those legal principles are described in this outline, as well as the outlines designed for Multistate Bar Examination preparation, including the Constitutional Law, Civil Procedure, and Evidence outlines.

The NCBE usually does not test local statutes or rules of court on the MPRE. However, be aware that some MPRE questions could "include the text of a local statute or rule that must be considered when answering that question." If you encounter such a question, use legal reasoning and analysis to apply the text of the given statute or rule in answering the question.

Coverage of the Outlines

This outline is intended to cover the main Rules and provisions of the Code and the Restatement that may be tested on the MPRE. Some of these legal principles may be more commonly tested than others. The other legal principles, however, remain subject to potentially being tested.

Due to the broad scope of the potentially testable issues and rules from sources beyond the Rules, Code, and Restatement, you might encounter a novel question not covered by these sources. Alternatively, you might encounter a question where the answer choice you anticipate is not presented to you. In those situations, use common sense, logic, and the process of elimination to select the best available answer choice. When attempting to eliminate incorrect answer choices, beware of answer choices that are factually accurate but legally incorrect.

MPRE STRATEGIES

Before taking a practice test or answering sample questions, you must learn:

- the testable provisions of the Rules, the Code, and the Restatement;

- the key words or phrases that may be used and underlined in the call of the question on the MPRE. Knowing the meaning of those words and phrases will enable you, when taking your own exam, to easily identify:

  - the type of question asked;
  - what the question is testing; and
  - what type of answer might be correct.

These words and phrases are described on the NCBE website, www.ncbex.org, and in NCBE testing materials. The NCBE provides MPRE Sample Questions, which are representative of the questions presented in an actual MPRE exam.

The multiple-choice questions on the MPRE always include four answer choices. Generally, there are two types of questions. One type simply provides a fact pattern and question and lists the four answer choices. Usually, this type of question is more common than the other type of question.

The other type of question provides a fact pattern and question, lists three or four statements, and then provides four answer choices asking which of the statements are correct. To answer this type of question, you will need to evaluate the statements and determine whether or not they are correct, and then choose the appropriate answer choice. The NCBE has not used this type of question in recent MPRE exams.

The fact patterns on the MPRE may include indented and quoted text. This text might be, for example, a person's verbal statement, contents of a document, or words used in a communication to the public. This type of information is at least as relevant as the rest of the fact pattern, and may contain facts that, when correctly analyzed under the controlling legal principles, will better enable you to select the correct answer.

Generally, most questions test one legal principle and/or its exception(s). Some questions might seem to test more than one legal principle, especially when the question arises in a factual context that relates to or is governed by other relevant legal principles. In this event, it is important to ascertain which legal principle is controlling when you are considering the answer choices and before you select an answer.

This is most likely to occur when the controlling legal principles are related, such as the duty of confidentiality in the context of a conflict of interest in representing multiple clients. Similarly, the legal principles governing the features of a retainer agreement and restrictions on contractually limiting liability for legal malpractice could apply simultaneously in a single factual situation.

Sometimes the same main legal principles are tested within different factual contexts, such as criminal, civil, or administrative proceedings. These types of legal principles include, for example, the duty of confidentiality and conflicts of interest in representing clients. Other legal principles, however, only apply in more limited contexts. For example, a few of the Rules regarding law firms only apply to a few specific contexts in which lawyers work together.

Some of the main issues and associated legal principles that are tested include:

- attorney advertising (including both media and content);
- competence in ordinary and emergency situations;
- conflicts of interest involving lawyers serving in the public and private sectors;
- disqualification of judges due to financial interests (including interests of immediate family and friends);
- false statements to anyone or any tribunal;
- fee sharing (division) with non-lawyers;
- assisting non-lawyers in the practice of law;
- agreements limiting malpractice liability;
- retainer agreements;
- contingency fees;
- publicity (literary) rights;
- prohibitions on attempting to influence judges and jurors;
- contacting unrepresented persons (e.g., using agents);
- public statements about judges (made by either lawyers or other candidates for judicial office);
- campaign contributions to judges or judicial candidates; and
- gifts to judges.

To succeed on the MPRE, you will need a practical working knowledge of how these legal principles apply to specific situations. For example, you should know how these legal principles apply to a lawyer's handling of personal funds, as well how those principles apply to funds received from clients and party-opponents. One important and testable issue is how to recognize and avoid the improper commingling of funds between the lawyer's general account and a client trust account.

Learning the controlling legal principles and how to pass the MPRE is more than an academic exercise. The MPRE tests issues that might arise in the real-life practice of law. For example, at least one state added the MPRE with the intent that it would reduce the problem of new attorneys violating the state's rules of professional ethics early in their careers after graduating from law school. In that sense, the MPRE's purpose could be considered as a preventative measure, and it serves an important function in making sure lawyers are educated about their professional responsibilities.

MPRE BASICS AND STRATEGIES

REVIEW QUESTIONS

1. The MPRE consists of:
   a. 50 questions, all of which count toward your final score.
   b. 60 questions, all of which count toward your final score.
   c. 50 questions, all but 10 of which count toward your final score.
   d. 60 questions, all but 10 of which count toward your final score.

2. The format of the MPRE includes:
   a. fact pattern questions with four possible answers from which you pick the best answer.
   b. true / false questions based on fact patterns from which you pick the best answer.
   c. fact pattern questions requiring short sentence answers.
   d. all of the above.

3. The MPRE tests:
   a. knowledge of state-specific ethics law regarding professional conduct.
   b. knowledge of established standards and rules related to a lawyer's professional conduct.
   c. reconciliation of personal ethical standards to model ethical rules.
   d. knowledge of proposed standards of professional conduct in the legal profession.

4. The sources of rules related to a lawyer's professional conduct that are tested on the MPRE include:
   a. generally established principles in the law of evidence and the Model Code of Judicial Conduct.
   b. generally established principles in the law of evidence and the ABA Model Rules of Professional Conduct.
   c. the ABA Model Rules of Professional Conduct and the Model Code of Judicial Conduct.
   d. generally established principles in the law of evidence, the Model Code of Judicial Conduct, and the ABA Model Rules of Professional Conduct.

5. An MPRE question sets forth a local rule governing the ethical conduct of a lawyer and asks for your analysis of the rule. You must analyze it using:
   a. the rules governing the locality in which the rule was promulgated.
   b. the state rules of professional responsibility.
   c. legal reasoning and analysis.
   d. ethical standards which follow local custom and usage.

6. On the MPRE, the phrase "subject to discipline" means the described conduct:

    a.   will result in an attorney or judge losing his or her license to practice law.

    b.   will subject the attorney or judge to a lawsuit.

    c.   shall result in sanction by the appropriate authority.

    d.   subjects the attorney or judge to discipline under the ABA Model Rules.

7. When the phrases "may" and "proper" are used in an MPRE question, the question is asking:
    a.   whether the court's permission is necessary before proceeding in an ethical manner.
    b.   if the conduct described is appropriate under local court rules.
    c.   if the conduct under consideration is professionally appropriate and would not subject the lawyer to discipline.
    d.   whether the conduct under consideration is a violation of the Canons of Ethics.

8. "Subject to litigation sanction," when used on the MPRE, means the conduct in question:
    a.   will subject the offending attorney to a dismissal of his client's case.
    b.   will subject the lay client to sanctions when the court discovers his unethical conduct.
    c.   will subject an attorney or an attorney's law firm to sanctions by the court.
    d.   will cause the judge to disqualify herself in order to avoid a conflict of interest and sanctions for continuing to preside over the litigation.

9. When appearing on the MPRE, the term "subject to disqualification" means:
    a.   the conduct described would subject a lawyer, but not the lawyer's firm, to disqualification as counsel in the case.
    b.   the conduct described would subject a lawyer, and/or the lawyer's firm, to disqualification as counsel in the case.
    c.   the conduct described would result in an immediate mistrial.
    d.   the conduct described would disqualify the attorney in question from ever practicing in that specific court.

10. If you see the term "subject to civil liability" on the MPRE, it means:
    a.   the conduct described could subject the lawyer or the lawyer's law firm to civil liability such as malpractice, breach of fiduciary duty, or misrepresentation.
    b.   the conduct described could subject the lawyer or the lawyer's firm to public sanction by the civil law authorities, such as censure, rebuke, or loss of license.
    c.   the conduct described could require the lawyer or the lawyer's firm to immediately withdraw from the case to maintain civility and avoid an appearance of impropriety.
    d.   the conduct described requires the judge to restore order in the court and find the offending attorney liable for contempt.

11. If you see the term "subject to criminal liability" on the MPRE, it means:
    a.   the conduct described bars the lawyer or firm from collecting fees in any case on which the lawyer or firm worked subsequent to the filing of a criminal charge against the lawyer or firm.

    b. the conduct described, if proven to be true, automatically subjects the lawyer or the lawyer's firm to the same penalty imposed against their criminal defendant client.

    c. the conduct described is a crime for which the attorney and/or the attorney's firm must be found liable as they are officers of the court and have presumptive knowledge of criminal law.

    d. the conduct described could subject the lawyer or firm to criminal liability such as aiding and abetting a criminal action, fraud, or obstruction of justice.

12. The "disciplining authority" of an attorney is:

    a. the attorney's supervisor within the law firm or, for a sole practitioner, the acting president of the local bar association.

    b. the local bar association's membership sitting in their regulatory capacity.

    c. the agency charged with regulating the legal profession, usually the state bar association.

    d. the prosecutor in the judicial district.

13. An attorney is referred to as a "certified specialist" if the attorney has:

    a. taken the proscribed number of continuing legal education credits in the specialization.

    b. served as an understudy to a certified specialist in the relevant specialization for at least 24 months.

    c. proven expertise to the chief justice of the state supreme court during an in-camera interview.

    d. been granted the certification by the appropriate regulatory authority.

14. The terms "informed consent" and "consent after consultation":

    a. have two separate and distinct meanings within the MPRE.

    b. mean the same thing on the MPRE.

    c. in criminal cases, have more serious ethical implications for an attorney due to the liberty interest of the client being at stake.

    d. must be explained by an attorney to a client under arrest and subject to custodial interrogation. Failure to explain the terms is an ethical violation.

MPRE BASICS AND STRATEGIES

ANSWERS TO REVIEW QUESTIONS

Answer 1

The correct answer is choice D. 50 questions count. There are 10 additional experimental questions. You cannot determine which questions count toward your score. Therefore, you should answer all the questions.

Answer 2

The correct answer is choice A. You must pick the "best" answer from four possible choices in response to a fact pattern question.

Answer 3

The correct answer is choice B. The MPRE tests knowledge of established standards and rules related to a lawyer's professional conduct.

Answer 4

The correct answer is choice D. Generally established principles in the law of evidence, the Model Code of Judicial Conduct, and the ABA Model Rules of Professional Conduct are all testable on the MPRE.

Answer 5

The correct answer is choice C. General legal reasoning and analysis should be used to analyze local rules or statutes presented on the MPRE.

Answer 6

The correct answer is choice D. Attorneys and judges are subject to discipline under the ABA Model Professional Rules of Conduct or Model Code of Judicial Conduct.

Answer 7

The correct answer is choice C. An MPRE question testing the appropriateness of a lawyer's conduct may ask "May an attorney do X or Y?" Alternatively, the question may ask "Is it proper for an attorney to do X or Y?"

Answer 8

The correct answer is choice C. A litigation sanction is a sanction imposed by a court during the course of litigation upon an attorney and/or the attorney's firm for inappropriate conduct. Such sanctions may include, but are not limited to, contempt, fine, fees, or disqualification.

Answer 9

The correct answer is choice B. Disqualification refers to counsel and/or the firm's inability to continue representing a client due to their conduct in violation of a relevant ethical rule.

Answer 10

The correct answer is choice A. An attorney or firm subject to civil liability is subject to legal action in civil court for violating a duty owed to a client.

Answer 11

The correct answer is choice D. An attorney or firm subject to criminal liability is subject to legal action in criminal court for violating criminal laws.

Answer 12

The correct answer is choice C. In most states, the state bar association has regulatory authority, including disciplinary authority, over members of the bar.

Answer 13

The correct answer is choice D. The present method of certification as a specialist is established by the appropriate authority regulating the practice of law within a state.

Answer 14

The correct answer is choice B. The terms "informed consent" and "consent after consultation" have the same meaning on the MPRE.

PROFESSIONAL RESPONSIBILITY

When studying the rules and standards governing lawyers' professional duties, you should pay special attention to whether a rule *requires* a lawyer to do something, or merely *recommends* or *permits* a lawyer to do something. The keywords "shall" and "must" indicate a required (or prohibited) action, while the keywords "should" and "may" indicate recommended or permitted actions.

I. REGULATION OF THE LEGAL PROFESSION

A. Powers of Courts and Other Bodies to Regulate Lawyers

When lawyers or parties are involved in court proceedings, their conduct is subject to judicial scrutiny, as well as some degree of judicial control. The judicial control serves to ensure and enforce compliance with ethical rules and other applicable legal provisions.

1) EXPRESS AUTHORITY

The Rules provide that the "ultimate authority over the legal profession is vested largely in the courts." Model Rules of Prof'l Conduct Preamble [10]. This authority is both *express* and *inherent*. Express authority includes enforcement of the Rules either in cases before the court, which could lead to disciplinary proceedings, or judicial review of determinations from disciplinary proceedings.

In addition to express legal authority, courts also possess certain inherent powers to regulate lawyers. Accordingly, the authority of courts to regulate is not necessarily limited to the express scope of legal provisions (such as rules of professional conduct or court rules). The courts' inherent powers to regulate lawyers flow from various sources.

2) INHERENT AUTHORITY

a) Officer of the Court

Lawyers are officers of the court and are subject to the courts' express and inherent authority to regulate them. Arguably, the Rules themselves provide a basis for a court's inherent authority to regulate lawyers. The Rules describe lawyers in many ways, including that they are "officer[s] of the legal system". Model Rules of Prof'l Conduct Preamble [1]

Specifically, as court officers, lawyers' legal and ethical responsibilities are not restricted to legal provisions, such as the Rules, that govern their conduct. Rather, the Rules and other legal provisions serve as the express basis of lawyers' responsibilities, but not as their limit. In other words, as court officers, lawyers must also fulfill additional inherent obligations and duties.

b) Professional Liability Standards

1

The courts' exercise of inherent authority has involved using the Rules in other ways, such as for guidance in establishing standards of legal malpractice liability, as illustrated below:

> As to whether ethical standards are admissible as some evidence of this standard of care, courts take four different approaches . . . . First, some courts hold that professional ethical standards conclusively establish the duty of care and any violation constitutes negligence per se. Second, a minority of courts finds that a professional ethical violation establishes a rebuttable presumption of legal malpractice. Third, a large majority of courts treats professional ethical standards as evidence of the common law duty of care. Finally, one court has found professional ethical standards inadmissible as evidence of an attorney's duty of care.

Allen v. Lefkoff, Duncan, Grimes & Dermer, P.C., 265 Ga. 374, 453 S.E.2d 719 (1995).

Such judicial treatment of the professional ethical standards is an example of the courts' exercise of the inherent power to regulate lawyers, rather than an example of the courts' express authority under the Rules. Using a Rule violation as the basis for civil liability is not an exercise of the courts' *express* power to regulate lawyers because the Rules "are designed to provide guidance to lawyers and to provide a structure for regulating conduct through disciplinary agencies. They are not designed to be a basis for civil liability. Nevertheless, since the Rules do establish standards of conduct by lawyers, a lawyer's violation of a Rule may be evidence of breach of the applicable standard of conduct." Model Rules of Prof'l Conduct Scope [20]. Therefore, the courts' use of the Rules as presumptions regarding civil liability, which is somewhat in conflict with the Rules themselves, could be considered the courts' exercise of its inherent power to regulate lawyers.

c) Additional Methods of Exercising Inherent Authority

Courts could also be said to exercise their inherent power to regulate lawyers when they take the following types of action (i.e., the following would be examples of the courts' inherent power if they are not acting pursuant to the Rules or any other express legal provision):

- holding lawyers in contempt;
- sanctioning lawyers by requiring them to relinquish legal fees; or
- dismissing an action.

B. Admission to the Profession

A non-attorney individual may apply for admission to the bar of a jurisdiction. Also, an attorney in one jurisdiction can apply for admission to the bar in another jurisdiction. The admissions process requires an applicant to file forms on which the applicant must make certain statements or disclosures. The Rules require that these statements be *truthful* and that these disclosures be *complete*.

★   1)   BAR ADMISSION

★★   a)   False Statements or Nondisclosures

An applicant for admission to the bar must not (1) knowingly make a false statement of material fact; or(2) fail to disclose a fact necessary to correct a misapprehension known by the applicant to have arisen in the matter; or (3) knowingly fail to respond to a lawful demand for information from an admissions or disciplinary authority. However, an applicant does not need to disclose information otherwise protected by Rule 1.6 (referred to as the "Rule of Confidentiality"), which is addressed later. Model Rules of Prof'l Conduct R. 8.1.

C.   Regulation After Admission

Once a lawyer is admitted to the state bar, the lawyer becomes subject to regulation under the Rules by the professional authority of the jurisdiction. Violation of the Rules may result in disciplinary action by the disciplinary authority of the jurisdiction.

        1)   ACTIONS SUBJECTING ATTORNEY TO DISCIPLINE

           a)   Violating the Rules

              (1)   Lawyer's Acts

As a general matter, a lawyer is subject to discipline when violating, or attempting to violate, the Rules.

              (2)   Acts of Other

A lawyer is also subject to discipline for knowingly assisting or inducing another person to do so, or do so through the acts of a third person, as when a lawyer requests or instructs an agent to violate the Rules on the lawyer's behalf. Model Rules of Prof'l Conduct R. 8.4 cmt. [1].

           b)   Criminal Actions

Although a lawyer is criminally liable for criminal law violations, a lawyer also faces professional consequences for offenses that indicate a lack of certain characteristics relevant to legal practice. Offenses involving violence, dishonesty, breach of trust, or serious interference with the administration of justice are in that category.

           c)   Actions Involving Dishonesty

A lawyer may not engage in any conduct involving dishonesty, fraud, deceit, or misrepresentation.

        2)   DISCIPLINARY MATTERS

★★   a)   Lawyer's False Statements or Nondisclosures

If a jurisdiction's professional authority commences proceedings against a lawyer, the lawyer must generally respond in writing. These forms or papers may require the lawyer to provide statements and disclosures with respect to a disciplinary matter. The Rules require that these statements be *truthful* and that these disclosures be *complete*.

A lawyer must not knowingly make a false statement of material fact in connection with a disciplinary matter. Also, a lawyer must not fail to disclose a fact necessary to correct a misapprehension known by the person to have arisen in the disciplinary matter, or knowingly fail to respond to a lawful demand for information from a disciplinary authority. This Rule does not require disclosure of information otherwise protected by the Rule of Confidentiality. Model Rules of Prof'l Conduct R. 8.1.

D.   Mandatory and Permissive Reporting of Professional Misconduct

A lawyer must report another lawyer's professional misconduct to a jurisdiction's professional authority.

★★★   1)   REPORTING PROFESSIONAL MISCONDUCT

                    a)   Lawyer and Lawyer

A lawyer who knows that another lawyer has committed a violation of the Rules that raises a substantial question as to that lawyer's honesty, trustworthiness, and fitness to act as a lawyer *must* inform the appropriate professional authority. Model Rules of Prof'l Conduct R. 8.3(a).

                    b)   Lawyer and Judge

Similarly, a lawyer who knows that a judge has committed a violation of the rules of judicial conduct that raises a substantial question as to the judge's fitness for office *must* inform the appropriate authority. Model Rules of Prof'l Conduct R. 8.3(b).

                    c)   Exceptions

The Rule does not require disclosure of information otherwise protected by the Rule of Confidentiality or information gained by a lawyer or judge while participating in an approved lawyer assistance program. Model Rules of Prof'l Conduct R. 8.3(c).

★★★★   2)   WHAT CONSTITUTES PROFESSIONAL MISCONDUCT

Any violation of the Rules could constitute professional misconduct. Additionally, the Rules list several additional types of professional misconduct. Specifically, it is professional misconduct for a lawyer to:

- violate the rules: violate or attempt to violate the Rules, knowingly assist or induce another to do so, or do so through the acts of another;

- commit a crime: commit a criminal act that reflects adversely on the lawyer's honesty, trustworthiness or fitness as a lawyer in other respects;
- perpetrate falsehoods: engage in conduct involving dishonesty, fraud, deceit or misrepresentation;
- prejudice justice: engage in conduct that is prejudicial to the administration of justice;
- represent improper influence: state or imply an ability to influence improperly a government agency or official or to achieve results by means that violate the Rules or other law; or
- assist unethical judicial conduct: knowingly assist a judge or judicial officer in conduct that is a violation of applicable rules of judicial conduct or other law.

Model Rules of Prof'l Conduct R. 8.4(a)-(f).

E. Unauthorized Practice of Law

As a general matter, a law school graduate who has not been admitted to the bar of a jurisdiction is not authorized to practice law in that jurisdiction until the graduate is admitted to the jurisdiction's bar. A lawyer who is admitted to practice law in one jurisdiction can only practice law in another jurisdiction in which the lawyer is not a member of the bar under certain limited circumstances provided by the Rules. The lawyer may violate the Rules by practicing law in another jurisdiction without proper authorization.

1)   UNAUTHORIZED PRACTICE OR ASSISTANCE OF UNAUTHORIZED PRACTICE OF LAW

A lawyer must not practice law in a jurisdiction in violation of the regulation of the legal profession in that jurisdiction, or assist another in doing so. Model Rules of Prof'l Conduct R. 5.5(a). An exception applies under limited circumstances when a lawyer who is admitted to the bar of one state seeks to temporarily provide legal services in another state in which the lawyer is not admitted. Model Rules of Prof'l Conduct R. 5.5(c). This limited admission to practice is referred to as "admission pro hac vice."

Note that a lawyer may assist a person who is representing himself. A person is generally permitted to represent himself, and, therefore, a lawyer assisting such a person is not assisting in the unauthorized practice of law.

F. Multijurisdictional Practice of Law

Under certain limited circumstances, a lawyer who is admitted to the bar in one United States jurisdiction, and not disbarred or suspended from practice in any jurisdiction, may provide legal services on a temporary basis in another jurisdiction. Model Rules of Prof'l Conduct R. 5.5(c).

1)   ASSOCIATION WITH LAWYER IN OTHER JURISDICTION

One such circumstance is when legal services are undertaken in association with a lawyer who is admitted to practice in the other jurisdiction and who actively participates in the matter. Model Rules of Prof'l Conduct R. 5.5(c)(1).

2) TRIBUNAL PROCEEDING

Another circumstance is when legal services are in, or reasonably related to, a pending or potential proceeding before a tribunal in the lawyer's jurisdiction or the other jurisdiction, if the lawyer, or a person the lawyer is assisting, is authorized by law or order to appear in such proceeding or reasonably expects to be so authorized. Model Rules of Prof'l Conduct R. 5.5(c)(2). Note that the Rules generally use the term tribunal when referring to a court or other similar decision-making authority such as the judicial body of an administrative agency.

3) ALTERNATIVE DISPUTE RESOLUTION PROCEEDING

A third circumstance is when legal services are related to a potential arbitration, mediation, or other alternative dispute resolution proceeding. A court may authorize an attorney to appear if the services are related to the lawyer's practice in a jurisdiction in which the lawyer is admitted to practice. Model Rules of Prof'l Conduct R. 5.5(c)(3).

4) OTHER CIRCUMSTANCES

A final circumstance is when other legal services are reasonably related to the lawyer's practice in a jurisdiction in which the lawyer is admitted to practice. Model Rules of Prof'l Conduct R. 5.5(c)(4).

★★ **G.   Fee Division with a Non-Lawyer**

A lawyer or a law firm must not share legal fees with a non-lawyer, except under the following circumstances.

First, an agreement by a lawyer with the lawyer's firm, partner, or associate may provide for the payment of money, over a reasonable period of time after the lawyer's death, to the lawyer's estate or to one or more specified persons. Model Rules of Prof'l Conduct R. 5.4(a)(1).

Second, a lawyer who purchases the practice of a deceased, disabled, or disappeared lawyer may, pursuant to the provisions of the Rule regarding the sale of a law practice, pay to the estate or other representative of that lawyer the agreed-upon purchase price. Model Rules of Prof'l Conduct R. 5.4(a)(2).

Third, a lawyer or law firm may include non-lawyer employees in a compensation or retirement plan, even though the plan is based in whole or in part on a profit-sharing arrangement. Model Rules of Prof'l Conduct R. 5.4(a)(3).

Fourth, a lawyer may share court-awarded legal fees with a non-profit organization that employed, retained, or recommended employment of the lawyer in the matter. Model Rules of Prof'l Conduct R. 5.4(a)(4).

H. Law Firm and Other Forms of Practice

Several Rules govern the professional conduct of lawyers in law firms. A "law firm" may include a lawyer or lawyers in a law partnership, a sole proprietorship, a professional corporation, or some other association authorized to practice law. Model Rules of Prof'l Conduct R. 1.0(c). In addition, a "law firm" includes lawyers employed in the legal department of an organization (e.g., a corporation) or a legal services organization. *Id.*

I. Responsibility of Partners, Managers, Supervisory and Subordinate Lawyers

1) LAW FIRMS AND ASSOCIATIONS

a) Responsibilities of Partners and Supervisory Lawyers

★   (1)   Measures of Complying with Rules

A partner in a law firm, or a lawyer who individually or together with other lawyers possesses comparable managerial authority in a law firm, must make reasonable efforts to ensure that the firm implements measures giving reasonable assurance that all lawyers in the firm conform to the Rules. Model Rules of Prof'l Conduct R. 5.1(a).

(a)   Scope of Application

The foregoing Rule applies to lawyers having managerial authority over the professional work of more than one lawyer in a partnership, professional corporation, or other association authorized to practice law. Model Rules of Prof'l Conduct R. 5.1 cmt. [1]. It also includes lawyers having comparable managerial authority in a legal services organization or a law department of an enterprise or government agency. *Id.*

(2)   Lawyer with Direct Supervisory Authority

A lawyer having direct supervisory authority over another lawyer must make reasonable efforts to ensure that the other lawyer conforms to the Rules of Professional Conduct. Model Rules of Prof'l Conduct R. 5.1(b).

(3)   Supervisory Lawyer's Responsibility for Another Lawyer's Violation

A supervisory lawyer will be responsible for a subordinate lawyer's violation of an ethical rule if: (1) the supervisory lawyer orders or, with knowledge of the specific conduct, ratifies the conduct involved; or (2) the supervisory lawyer is a partner or has comparable managerial authority in the law firm in which the other lawyer practices, or has direct supervisory authority over the other lawyer, and knows of the conduct at a time when its consequences can be avoided or mitigated but fails to take reasonable remedial action. Model Rules of Prof'l Conduct R. 5.1(c).

 b) Responsibilities Regarding Non-Lawyer Assistants

As a general principle, a supervisory lawyer is also responsible for an action by a non-lawyer assistant that violates the Rules if either prong of the foregoing test is satisfied. Model Rules of Prof'l Conduct R. 5.3(c).

Specifically, a supervisory lawyer must make reasonable efforts to ensure that the non-lawyer's conduct is compatible with the professional obligations of the lawyer. Model Rules of Prof'l Conduct R. 5.3(b). A lawyer will be responsible for a non-lawyer's conduct that would constitute a violation of the Rules if engaged in by a lawyer if: (1) the lawyer orders or, with the knowledge of the specific conduct, ratifies the conduct involved; or (2) the lawyer is a partner or has comparable managerial authority in the law firm in which the person is employed, or has direct supervisory authority over the person, and knows of the conduct at a time when its consequences can be avoided or mitigated but fails to take reasonable remedial action. Model Rules of Prof'l Conduct R. 5.3(c). For example, a supervisory lawyer would be responsible for a paralegal's shredding of documents pursuant to the lawyer's instruction. Paralegals are paraprofessional legal assistants.

c) Responsibilities of a Subordinate Lawyer

As a general principle, a lawyer may not escape responsibility for ethical violations simply because the lawyer acted at someone else's direction. Specifically, a lawyer is bound by the Rules even when the lawyer acted at the direction of another person. Model Rules of Prof'l Conduct R. 5.2(a). A subordinate lawyer does not violate the Rules, however, if that lawyer acts in accordance with a supervisory lawyer's reasonable resolution of a question of professional duty. Model Rules of Prof'l Conduct R. 5.2(b).

d) Professional Independence of a Lawyer

★ **(1) Forming Partnership with Non-Lawyer**

A lawyer cannot form a partnership with a non-lawyer if *any* activities of the partnership consist of the practice of law. Model Rules of Prof'l Conduct R. 5.4(b).

★ **(2) Lawyer's Professional Judgment**

A lawyer must not permit a person who recommends, employs, or pays the lawyer to render legal services for another, to direct or regulate the lawyer's professional judgment in rendering such legal services. Model Rules of Prof'l Conduct R. 5.4(c). For example, if a parent pays for the legal services of a child, the lawyer cannot permit the parent to direct or regulate the lawyer's professional judgment.

★

(3)   Involvement of Non-Lawyer

A lawyer must not practice with, or in the form of, a professional corporation or association authorized to practice law for a profit, if a non-lawyer:

- owns any interest therein, *except* that a fiduciary representative of the estate of a lawyer may hold the stock or interest of the lawyer for a reasonable time during administration;
- is a director or officer thereof, or occupies the position of similar responsibility in any form of association; or
- has the right to direct or control the professional judgment of a lawyer.

Model Rules of Prof'l Conduct R. 5.4(d).

J.   Restrictions on Right to Practice

The Rules govern the type and nature of contractual restrictions that can be imposed upon a lawyer within a relationship between the lawyer and others.

★★   1)   RESTRICTIONS ON RIGHT TO PRACTICE

a)   Employment or Other Relationship

A lawyer must not participate in offering or making a partnership, shareholders, operating, employment, or other similar type of agreement that restricts the right of a lawyer to practice after termination of the relationship, except an agreement concerning benefits upon retirement. Model Rules of Prof'l Conduct R. 5.6(a).

b)   Settlement of a Client Controversy

A lawyer must not participate in offering or making an agreement in which a restriction on the lawyer's right to practice is part of the settlement of a client controversy. Model Rules of Prof'l Conduct R. 5.6(b).

REGULATION OF THE LEGAL PROFESSION

REVIEW QUESTIONS

1. Authority to regulate attorney conduct comes from:
   a. a state's supreme court's published rules of attorney conduct.
   b. mandatory membership in the state bar association which requires adherence to its charter and bylaws.
   c. the Rules of Professional Conduct, express and inherent judicial powers, and all courts' supervisory roles over attorneys acting as officers of the court.
   d. the ABA's charter and bylaws.

2. The ABA's Rules of Professional Conduct are:
   a. the starting point of legal responsibilities.
   b. the end goal of legal responsibilities.
   c. the mandatory path to acting in a legally responsible manner.
   d. the recommended path to acting in a legally responsible manner.

3. A lawyer may not be involved in any conduct involving:
   a. gambling, vice, or morally reprehensible activities.
   b. public intoxication resulting in disturbing the peace.
   c. government-identified terrorist organizations.
   d. dishonesty, fraud, deceit, or misrepresentation.

4. A lawyer must reply to all disciplinary actions against her:
   a. within two business days of receiving notice of them.
   b. truthfully and completely.
   c. immediately and without excuse.
   d. personally and not through legal counsel.

5. A lawyer must report another lawyer's alleged professional misconduct involving:
   a. honesty, trustworthiness, and fitness to act as a lawyer.
   b. questionable moral judgment.
   c. the lawyer's family problems.
   d. the lawyer's contemplation of filing bankruptcy.

6. The following action constitutes professional misconduct:
   a. being arrested for a crime that does not involve dishonesty.
   b. being convicted of driving while under the influence of alcohol or drugs.

    c. inducing another attorney to engage in a highly risky business venture.

    d. attempting to violate the Rules of Professional Conduct but not actually violating them.

7. A person is authorized to practice law when they are:

    a. admitted to the state bar.

    b. sworn in by the Chief Justice of the state Supreme Court.

    c. appearing for the first time in practice before a court.

    d. in actual possession of a license to practice law.

8. An attorney filing a Motion to Appear Pro Hoc Vice is an attorney's request to:

    a. appear before a court to contest a client's appearance on vice charges.

    b. bring the person(s) alleged to be involved in a vice crime before the court for questioning.

    c. appear before and practice in a court in a jurisdiction in which the attorney is not admitted.

    d. appear before a disciplinary committee to contest alleged misconduct.

9. Fee splitting by a lawyer with a non-lawyer is strictly prohibited under the following except:

    a. the lawyer and non-lawyer are married and share all income equally.

    b. the lawyer and non-lawyer have executed a fee splitting agreement and filed the same as a matter of public record and provided a copy to the appropriate disciplinary authority for review.

    c. the non-lawyer is a licensed securities dealer or investment advisor working to further the financial interests of the lawyer and the lawyer's clients.

    d. the lawyer pays the estate of a deceased lawyer a sum negotiated as the purchase price for the deceased lawyer's practice.

10. A lawyer with supervisory authority over another lawyer is responsible for the subordinate lawyer's violation of the Rules of Professional Conduct:

    a. even if the supervising lawyer is unaware of the unethical conduct as the supervising lawyer is always responsible for the actions of a subordinate lawyer.

    b. in all circumstances due to the supervising lawyer's role as a supervisor.

    c. if the supervising lawyer knows of or ratifies the unethical conduct, or if the supervising lawyer has direct supervisory authority over the subordinate lawyer and knows of the unethical conduct at a time when the supervisory lawyer could avoid or mitigate the unethical conduct but fails to do so.

    d. even if the supervising lawyer is assured in writing by the subordinate lawyer that the subordinate lawyer's actions are in full compliance with the Rules of

Professional Conduct.

11. A subordinate lawyer is bound by Rules of Professional Conduct even when directed by a supervising lawyer, but the subordinate lawyer will not be subject to discipline for violating those rules when:
    a. the subordinate lawyer informs the supervising lawyer of the possible violation of ethical rules but proceeds with the action.
    b. the subordinate lawyer informs the supervising lawyer of the possible violation of ethical rules and the supervising lawyer threatens to terminate the lawyer's employment unless the lawyer proceeds with the action.
    c. the subordinate lawyer acts in accordance with the supervising lawyer's reasonable resolution of a question of professional duty.
    d. the supervising lawyer takes full responsibility in writing for all actions and consequences of the subordinate lawyer's actions.

12. No third-party may direct a lawyer's professional, independent decision-making process and, therefore, a lawyer may not:
    a. enter into a business relationship with a non-lawyer if the business involves the practice of law or enter into any business form if a non-lawyer owns any interest in the business.
    b. invest in any business run by a non-lawyer that provides legal products or services outside of the lawyer's own practice.
    c. earn profit from a business the lawyer sold prior to being licensed to practice law but in which the lawyer, as part of the sale agreement, is to be paid a percentage of future profits by the new owner, a non-lawyer.
    d. marry an accountant who has sole control of the law firm's financial matters.

13. When a third-party pays for a lawyer to represent a client, the lawyer must:
    a. give adequate consideration to the third-party's opinion but make independent decisions with respect to actions taken for the client.
    b. give no consideration to the paying third-party who is not the client.
    c. abide by the client's wishes unless the client is a minor and the third-party is the minor's parent with authority and control over the client.
    d. abide by the third party's direction insofar as it does not harm the client.

14. If a lawyer enters into an agreement that restricts the lawyer's ability to practice law as a condition of a settlement in a breach of contract action with another local law firm, the lawyer is:
    a. not violating ethical rules because the lawyer may choose when and where to practice law.

b. violating ethical rules because the lawyer may not enter into any agreement that may restrict the lawyer's ability to practice law.

c. violating ethical rules because the lawyer may not enter into any agreement that may restrict the ability to practice law, except a retiring attorney may agree to limit the right to practice law in exchange for retirement benefits from the law firm.

d. not violating ethical rules because the attorney is exercising a constitutional right to free association.

REGULATION OF THE LEGAL PROFESSION

ANSWERS TO REVIEW QUESTIONS

Answer 1

The correct answer is choice C. Authority to regulate attorney conduct comes from three sources: 1) the Rules of Professional Conduct, 2) inherent judicial powers, and 3) all courts' regulatory roles over attorneys acting as officers of the court.

Answer 2

The correct answer is choice A. The ABA Rules of Professional Conduct are the starting point for legal responsibilities of a lawyer.

Answer 3

The correct answer is choice D. A lawyer may not be involved in any conduct involving dishonesty, fraud, deceit, or misrepresentation.

Answer 4

The correct answer is choice B. A lawyer must reply truthfully and completely to all disciplinary actions against her.

Answer 5

The correct answer is choice A. A lawyer's alleged professional misconduct involving honesty, trustworthiness, and fitness to act as a lawyer must be reported by another lawyer aware of the alleged professional misconduct.

Answer 6

The correct answer is choice D. Violating or attempting to violate the Rules of Professional Responsibility, knowingly assisting or inducing another lawyer to do so, or knowingly assisting or inducing a judge to violate the Code of Judicial Conduct always constitutes professional misconduct.

Answer 7

The correct answer is choice A. A person is authorized to practice law within a jurisdiction when they are admitted to that jurisdiction's bar.

Answer 8

The correct answer is choice C. An attorney who files a Motion to Appear Pro Hoc Vice requests that the court allow the attorney to appear and practice before that court for a limited time and purpose if the attorney is not admitted to practice in that jurisdiction.

Answer 9

The correct answer is choice D. Fee splitting by a lawyer with non-lawyers is allowed if the lawyer pays the estate of a deceased lawyer a sum negotiated as the purchase price for the deceased lawyer's practice, payments to non-lawyers are made over time after a lawyer's death as part of the estate, or non-lawyer employees are paid in a compensation or retirement plan based in part on a profit-sharing arrangement.

Answer 10

The correct answer is choice C. A lawyer with supervisory authority over another lawyer is responsible for the subordinate lawyer's violation of the Rules of Professional Conduct if: 1) the supervising lawyer knows of or ratifies the unethical conduct; or 2) if the supervising lawyer has direct supervisory authority over the subordinate lawyer and knows of the unethical conduct at a time when the supervisory lawyer could avoid or mitigate the unethical conduct but fails to do so.

Answer 11

The correct answer is choice C. A subordinate lawyer will not be subject to discipline for violating the Rules of Professional Conduct if the subordinate lawyer acts in accordance with the supervising lawyer's reasonable resolution of a question of professional duty.

Answer 12

The correct answer is choice A. No third-party may direct a lawyer's professional, independent decision-making process; therefore, a lawyer may not enter into a business relationship with a non-lawyer if the business involves the practice of law or enter into any business form if a non-lawyer owns any interest in the business.

Answer 13

The correct answer is choice B. The fact that a third-party refers or even pays for legal services for another person does not allow the lawyer to follow the direction of that third-party who is not the lawyer's client.

Answer 14

The correct answer is choice C. A lawyer may not enter into an agreement that may restrict the lawyer's ability to practice law, except a retiring attorney may agree to limit the right to practice law in exchange for retirement benefits from the law firm.

II.   THE CLIENT-LAWYER RELATIONSHIP

A.   Formation of Client-Lawyer Relationship

1)   MUTUAL AGREEMENT

A client-lawyer relationship is created when a person expresses to a lawyer the person's intent that the lawyer provide legal services for the person, and the lawyer expresses to the person consent to provide legal services. Restatement of the Law Governing Lawyers, Third, § 14(1)(a).

As a general matter, a lawyer usually can exercise discretion in deciding whether to represent a person who requests the lawyer's representation. This principle, however, is subject to exceptions, such as when a court orders a lawyer to represent a criminal defendant. Restatement of the Law Governing Lawyers, Third, § 14(2).

a)   Accepting Appointments

Under the Rules, a lawyer must not seek to avoid appointment by a tribunal to represent a person, except for good cause. Good cause would exist if:

- representing the client is likely to result in violation of the Rules or other law;
- representing the client is likely to result in an unreasonable financial burden on the lawyer; or
- the client or the cause is so repugnant to the lawyer as to be likely to impair the client-lawyer relationship or the lawyer's ability to represent the client.

Model Rules of Prof'l Conduct R. 6.2.

b)   Detrimental Reliance

Another way a client-lawyer relationship might form is if, after a client requests representation, the lawyer does not express any opposition to being hired and it would have been reasonable for the lawyer to have declined this representation. In such a situation, the lawyer would be obligated to represent the client who reasonably and detrimentally relied upon being represented by the lawyer and consequently did not procure the services of another lawyer. Restatement of the Law Governing Lawyers, Third, § 14(1)(b).

The Restatement summarizes this requirement by stating that a client-lawyer relationship arises when a person manifests to the lawyer the person's intent that the lawyer provide legal services for the person and the lawyer fails to manifest a lack of consent to do so, but the lawyer knows or reasonably should know that the person reasonably relies on the lawyer to provide the services. *Id.*

(1)   Example

Suppose a potential client contacts a domestic relations law firm. In response to the client's request for legal representation at an emergency child custody hearing in two weeks, a lawyer takes the potential client's paperwork and assures the client not to worry about the hearing. During the next 11 days, neither the lawyer nor the law firm contacts the potential client, who does not contact them or any other lawyers. The lawyer calls the potential client on the 12th day and declines the representation. In this situation, a court could find that a client-lawyer relationship exists based on the lawyer's delayed expression of an absence of intent to be retained.

2) ETHICAL CONSIDERATIONS FOR ACCEPTING CLIENTS

Some of the Rules provide guidance as to when a lawyer can accept or reject representation of a client. A lawyer should know, consider, and apply these Rules when making a discretionary decision whether to accept or reject the representation of a potential client. For example, a lawyer should reject representation of a client if the lawyer lacks the requisite legal competence to handle the matter. Model Rules of Prof'l Conduct R. 1.1. Similarly, the Rules prohibiting lawyers from counseling a client to engage in, or assisting a client with, criminal or fraudulent conduct relate to whether or not a lawyer may represent a client. Model Rules of Prof'l Conduct R. 1.2(a). Also, the Rules regarding conflict of interest are controlling with respect to whether a lawyer may represent a client if doing so would result in a conflict of interest. Model Rules of Prof'l Conduct Rs. 1.7-1.12.

A lawyer can accept representation of a client even if the lawyer thinks that the client will not succeed in a matter. Accordingly, a lawyer should not reject representation of a potential client on the basis of the lawyer's personal opposition to the client's legal position. However, a lawyer should reject representation of a potential client if the matter is completely baseless. Model Rules of Prof'l Conduct R. 3.1.

B. Scope, Objective, and Means of the Representation

1) SCOPE OF REPRESENTATION AND ALLOCATION OF AUTHORITY

a) General Considerations

Both the lawyer and client have authority and responsibility with respect to the objectives and means of the legal representation. In order to analyze the allocation of authority between client and lawyer, one would use the "objectives versus means" test. Annotated Model Rules of Professional Conduct, Rule 1.2, p. 36 (Sixth ed., ABA Center for Professional Responsibility).

(1) Client Decides Objectives of Representation

The client has ultimate authority to determine the objectives to be served by legal representation. For example, the client makes the final decision about whether to commence a cause of action or settle a civil matter.

A lawyer must abide by a client's decisions concerning the objectives of representation. Model Rules of Prof'l Conduct R. 1.2(a). In a criminal case, the lawyer must abide by the client's decision, after consultation with the lawyer, regarding:

- what plea will be entered,
- whether to waive a jury trial, and
- whether the client will testify. *Id.*

(2)   Lawyer Decides Means for Objectives

The lawyer must consult with the client regarding the means (e.g., technical, legal, and tactical matters) for pursuing the client's objectives. A lawyer ultimately decides the means for pursuing the objectives.

(3)   Lawyer Has Implied Authority to Act for Client

The lawyer may act as is impliedly authorized to represent the client. Model Rules of Prof'l Conduct R. 1.2(a).

b)   Client with Diminished Capacity

When a client's capacity to make adequately considered decisions in connection with representation is diminished, whether because of minority status, mental impairment, or for some other reason, the lawyer must, as far as reasonably possible, maintain a normal client-lawyer relationship with the client. Model Rules of Prof'l Conduct R. 1.14(a).

If a lawyer reasonably believes that the client has diminished capacity, is at risk of substantial physical, financial or other harm unless action is taken, and cannot adequately act in the client's own interest, the lawyer may take reasonably necessary protective action, including consulting with individuals or entities that have the ability to take action to protect the client and, in appropriate cases, seeking the appointment of a guardian *ad litem*, conservator, or guardian. Model Rules of Prof'l Conduct R. 1.14(b).

Information relating to the representation of a client with diminished capacity is protected by the Rule regarding confidentiality. When taking reasonably necessary protective action, the lawyer is impliedly authorized under the Rule of confidentiality to reveal information about the client to the extent reasonably necessary to protect the client's interests. *Id.* Model Rules of Prof'l Conduct R. 1.14(c).

C.   Decision-Making Authority – Actual and Apparent

1)   ALLOCATION OF AUTHORITY

A client and a lawyer may generally agree as to which of them will make certain decisions, and the client may instruct the lawyer during representation. Restatement of the Law Governing

Lawyers, Third, § 21(1)-(2). A lawyer may use any lawful means to advance the client's objectives. *Id.* at § 21(3).

a) Authority Always Reserved to Client

A client in a civil matter always has authority to decide on settlement of a claim and whether to appeal. *Id.* at § 22(1). A defendant in a criminal case has authority to decide on making a plea, having a jury trial, testifying, and whether to appeal. *Id.*

b) Authority Always Reserved to Lawyer

A lawyer has authority, which neither a client agreement nor instruction can trump: 1) to decline performing, counseling, or assisting with acts that the lawyer reasonably believes to be unlawful; and 2) to take actions or make decisions in the representation that the lawyer reasonably believes are required by law or court order. *Id.* at § 23(1).

2) WHEN LAWYER HAS ACTUAL OR APPARENT AUTHORITY

a) Lawyer's Actual Authority

A lawyer has actual authority to act for a client when:

- the act is always reserved to the lawyer (as described above);
- the client has actually authorized the lawyer to act; or
- the client has ratified (subsequently consented to) the act.

Id. at § 26.

b) Lawyer's Apparent Authority

A lawyer has apparent authority to act for a client if a tribunal or the third party *reasonably assumes* that the lawyer is authorized to do the act based on the client's expressions of such authorization. *Id.* at § 27 (emphasis added).

★
★

D. Counsel and Assistance Within the Bounds of the Law

As a general matter, a lawyer's assistance to a client cannot go beyond the limits of the law. A lawyer cannot counsel a client to engage in, or assist a client in, conduct that the lawyer knows is criminal or fraudulent. Model Rules of Prof'l Conduct R. 1.2(d). However, a lawyer may discuss the legal consequences of any proposed course of conduct with a client. *Id.* A lawyer may also counsel or assist a client to make a good faith effort to determine the validity, scope, meaning, or application of the law. *Id.*

★★★

E. Termination of the Client-Lawyer Relationship

1) DECLINING OR TERMINATING REPRESENTATION

Termination or withdrawal of legal representation may be either mandatory (i.e., required) or permissive (i.e., voluntary).

a) Discharge by Lawyer--Mandatory Withdrawal

Generally, a lawyer cannot represent a client or, if representation has commenced, *must* withdraw from the representation of a client if:

- the representation will result in violation of the Rules or other law;
- the lawyer's physical or mental condition materially impairs the lawyer's ability to represent the client; or
- the lawyer is discharged.

Model Rules of Prof'l Conduct R. 1.16(a).

b) Discharge by Lawyer--Permissive Withdrawal

An alternative to mandatory withdrawal by a lawyer is permissive withdrawal. The lawyer *may* withdraw from representation in some circumstances. For example, a lawyer can withdraw representation if:

- withdrawal can be accomplished without material adverse effect on the client's interests;
- the client persists in a course of action involving the lawyer's services that the lawyer reasonably believes is criminal or fraudulent;
- the client has used the lawyer's services to perpetrate a crime or fraud;
- the client insists upon taking action that the lawyer considers repugnant or with which the lawyer has a fundamental disagreement;
- the client fails substantially to fulfill an obligation to the lawyer regarding the lawyer's services and has been given reasonable warning that the lawyer will withdraw unless the obligation is fulfilled;
- the representation will result in an unreasonable financial burden on the lawyer or has been rendered unreasonably difficult by the client; or
- other good cause exists for withdrawal.

Model Rules of Prof'l Conduct R. 1.16(b).

(1) Obligation to Tribunal

A lawyer must comply with applicable law requiring notice to or permission of a tribunal when terminating a representation, and when ordered to do so by a tribunal, a lawyer must continue representation notwithstanding good cause for terminating the representation. Model Rules of Prof'l Conduct R. 1.16(c). In other words, a tribunal (e.g., court) may refuse to allow an attorney to withdraw from a representation.

2) DISCHARGE BY CLIENT

The client-lawyer relationship can be terminated at the will of a client; however, a lawyer may be entitled to quasi-contract damages (i.e., unjust enrichment and promissory estoppel). Model Rules of Prof'l Conduct R. 1.16 cmt. [4].

3) DUTIES UPON DISCHARGE

As a general matter, the client's position should not be jeopardized by withdrawal. A lawyer must take steps to the extent reasonably practicable to protect a client's interests, such as:

- giving reasonable notice to the client,
- allowing time for employment of other counsel,
- surrendering files, papers and property to which the client is entitled, and
- refunding any advance payment (i.e., retainer) of a fee that has not been earned or incurred.

Model Rules of Prof'l Conduct R. 1.16(d).

A lawyer may retain papers relating to the client to the extent permitted by other law. *Id.*

F. Client-Lawyer Contracts

1) GENERAL RULE

The Restatement provides that a contract between a client and lawyer regarding their relationship, including a contract modifying an existing contract, usually can be enforced by either of them if the contract meets all applicable requirements. Restatement of the Law Governing Lawyers, Third, § 18(1). The client, however, may be able avoid the contract under certain circumstances.

a) Exception for Subsequent Formation or Modification

If the contract or modification is made more than a reasonable time after the lawyer has commenced representation of a client, the client can avoid the contract *unless* the lawyer shows that the contract and circumstances of its formation were fair and reasonable to the client. *Id.*

b) Exception for Post-Representation Formation

If the contract is made after the lawyer has finished providing services, the client can avoid the contract if the client was not informed of the facts needed to evaluate the appropriateness of the lawyer's compensation or other benefits conferred on the lawyer by the contract. *Id.*

c) Interpretation of Contract – Reasonable Person Standard

A tribunal should construe a contract between a client and a lawyer as a reasonable person in the client's circumstances would have construed it. Restatement of the Law Governing Lawyers, Third, § 18(2).

2) AGREEMENTS LIMITING CLIENT OR LAWYER DUTIES

a) Lawyer and Client Can Limit Lawyer's Duties

A client and lawyer may agree to reasonably limit a duty the lawyer would otherwise owe to the client if: 1) the client is adequately informed and consents; and 2) the terms of the limitation are reasonable given the circumstances. Restatement of the Law Governing Lawyers, Third, § 19(1).

b) Lawyer Can Waive Client's Duties

A lawyer may also agree to waive a client's duty to pay or other duty owed to the lawyer. Restatement of the Law Governing Lawyers, Third, § 19(2).

G. Communications with Client

1) DUTY TO INFORM AND CONSULT WITH CLIENT

In general, reasonable communication between a lawyer and client is necessary for the client to participate effectively in the representation. Model Rules of Prof'l Conduct R. 1.4 cmt. [1]. In particular, a lawyer must:

- promptly inform the client of any decision or circumstance for which the client's informed consent is required;
- reasonably consult with the client about the means by which the client's objectives are to be accomplished;
- keep a client reasonably informed about the status of the matter, including significant developments relating to the representation;
- promptly comply with reasonable requests for information and copies of significant documents to keep the client so informed; and
- consult with the client about any relevant limitation on the lawyer's conduct when the lawyer knows that the client expects assistance not permitted by the Rules or other law.

Model Rules of Prof'l Conduct R. 1.4(a).

Additionally, a lawyer must explain a matter to the extent reasonably necessary to enable the client to make an informed decision regarding the representation. Model Rules of Prof'l Conduct R. 1.4(b).

H. Fees

1) FEE AGREEMENTS

a)   General Principles

Fees for legal services are set by agreement between the lawyer and client. The agreement must be in writing and clearly set forth the terms of the representation. The fee must be reasonable under the totality of the circumstances, including the time, skill, and labor required. The fee should be set at the commencement of the representation or shortly thereafter. The fee cannot be unconscionable.

b)   Reasonable Fee Requirement

A lawyer cannot make an agreement for, charge, or collect an unreasonable fee or unreasonable amount for expenses. The factors to be considered when determining the reasonableness of a fee include, but are not limited to:

- the time and labor required;
- the novelty and difficulty of the questions involved;
- the skill required to perform the legal service properly;
- the likelihood, if apparent to the client, that the acceptance of the particular employment will preclude other employment by the lawyer;
- the fee customarily charged in the locality for similar legal services;
- the amount involved and the results obtained;
- the time limitations imposed by the client or by the circumstances;
- the nature and length of the professional relationship with the client;
- the experience, reputation, and ability of the lawyer doing the work; and
- whether the fee is fixed or contingent.

Model Rules of Prof'l Conduct R. 1.5(a).

c)   Communications Regarding Fees

Generally, the scope of the representation, the basis or rate of the fee, and the expenses for which the client will be responsible must be communicated to the client, preferably in writing, before or within a reasonable time after commencing the representation. Model Rules of Prof'l Conduct R. 1.5(b). This Rule, however, does not apply when a lawyer regularly represents a client and charges the same basis or rate each time. *Id.* In either case, any changes in the basis or rate of the fee or expenses must be communicated to the client. *Id.*

2)   CONTINGENCY FEES

a)   Prohibited for Criminal and Domestic Matters

Contingency fees are generally permissible, except in criminal or domestic relations cases. Model Rules of Prof'l Conduct R. 1.5(c)-(d). Specifically, a lawyer must not enter into an arrangement for, charge, or collect: (1) a contingent fee for representing a defendant in criminal case; or (2) any fee in a domestic relations matter, the payment or amount of which is contingent upon the securing of a divorce or upon the amount of alimony or support, or property settlement in lieu thereof. Model Rules of Prof'l Conduct R. 1.5(d).

b) Contingency Fee Agreements

A contingent fee agreement must be in writing and signed by the client and must state the method by which the fee is to be determined, including:

- the percentage or percentages that will accrue to the lawyer in the event of settlement, trial, or appeal;
- litigation and other expenses to be deducted from the recovery, and
- whether such expenses are to be deducted before or after the contingent fee is calculated.

Model Rules of Prof'l Conduct R. 1.5(c).

The agreement must clearly notify the client of any expenses for which the client will be liable, regardless of whether the client is the prevailing party. *Id.* Upon conclusion of a contingent fee matter, the lawyer must provide the client with a written statement describing the outcome of the matter and, if there is a recovery, showing the remittance to the client and the method of its determination. *Id.*

★ ### 3) FEE SPLITTING WITH OTHER LAWYERS

Under the Rules, a division of a fee between lawyers who are not in the same firm is permissible only if:

- the division is in proportion to the services performed by each lawyer or each lawyer assumes joint responsibility for the representation;
- the client agrees to the arrangement, including the share each lawyer will receive, and the agreement is confirmed in writing; and
- the total fee is reasonable.

Model Rules of Prof'l Conduct R. 1.5(e).

I. Sale of Law Practice

A lawyer or law firm can sell or purchase a law practice under the following circumstances:

- the seller ceases to engage in the private practice of law, or in the area of practice that has been sold, in the geographic area or in the jurisdiction in which the practice has been conducted;
- the entire practice, or the entire area of practice, is sold to one or more lawyers or law firms;
- client fees are not increased by reason of the sale;

- the seller gives written notice to each of the seller's clients regarding: (1) the proposed sale; (2) the client's right to retain other counsel or to take possession of the file; and (3) the fact that the client's consent will be presumed if the client takes no action within ninety days of receipt of the notice. If a client cannot be provided with notice, representation of the client may be transferred to the purchaser only upon entry of a court order.

Model Rules of Prof'l Conduct R. 1.17.

REGULATION OF THE LEGAL PROFESSION

REVIEW QUESTIONS

1. A lawyer does not have to represent any client unless appointed by a court to do so in a criminal case. Even then, the lawyer may refuse to represent the client for good cause shown if:
    a. the lawyer knows, beyond all reasonable doubt, that the client is guilty.
    b. the lawyer will lose potential business in the community.
    c. the client or the cause is so repugnant to the lawyer as to likely impair the lawyer-client relationship or representation of the client, or representing the client would violate the Rules of Professional Conduct or the law, or cause the lawyer undue financial burden.
    d. other lawyers in the firm unanimously oppose the lawyer's representation of a particular defendant.

2. A lawyer should reject representation of a client if:
    a. the client has committed a heinous act that offends the lawyer.
    b. the client asks the lawyer to seek payment for legal fees from friends and family members more than one time.
    c. the client's flirtatious spouse repeatedly distracts the lawyer's attention from the client.
    d. the position of the client is legally baseless.

3. The ultimate authority to determine the objectives of any legal representation rests with:
    a. the lawyer.
    b. the client.
    c. the lawyer and client together.
    d. the person paying the lawyer's fees.

4. In a criminal case, the lawyer must abide by the client's decision regarding:
    a. how to cross-examine a hostile witness personally known to the client.
    b. whether the client will testify and whether to waive a jury trial.
    c. whether to engage in reciprocal discovery after the defendant's discovery motion is granted.
    d. the percentage of fees to be paid if the client pleads guilty by reason of mental disease or defect.

5. If an attorney represents a client with diminished capacity, the lawyer must attempt to maintain a normal lawyer-client relationship with the client. If the lawyer reasonably believes the client is at risk of substantial physical, financial, or other harm, the lawyer may take reasonably necessary protective action such as seeking a guardian or conservator. When taking protective action, a lawyer is:

    a. implicitly authorized to reveal information about the client, but only to the extent reasonably necessary to protect the client's interest.

    b. implicitly authorized to request a court to remove the lawyer from the representation and appoint an attorney with specialty expertise to handle the matters involving the client's diminished capacity.

    c. explicitly authorized to take all reasonable actions to protect the client.

    d. explicitly authorized to hire additional professionals and attorneys to address the special needs of the client.

6. When a lawyer discusses with a client a course of criminal conduct being contemplated by the client, the lawyer:
    a. must advise the client to cease such communications lest the lawyer be forced to turn the client over to a law enforcement authority.
    b. may discuss with a client the nature and ramifications of the proposed criminal conduct.
    c. should dissuade the client from profiting or otherwise improving the client's legal situation by such conduct.
    d. may ignore such proposed criminal conduct as the discussion of any such conduct is protected by the lawyer-client privilege.

7. A lawyer must withdraw or decline representation of a client if:
    a. the client's physical or mental condition impairs representation.
    b. the lawyer's physical or mental condition impairs representation.
    c. the client files a complaint against the lawyer with a disciplinary authority.
    d. the lawyer was previously romantically involved with the client.

8. A lawyer may withdraw from representing a client if:
    a. good cause for withdrawal exists or, even if good cause for withdrawal does not exist, the lawyer's withdrawal from representation has no material adverse effect on the client's interest.
    b. the lawyer secures another client who pays substantially more and will require greater time and attention.
    c. legal representation becomes more difficult due to the client's bad temperament.
    d. the client fails to appear for appointments with the lawyer.

9. If ordered by a court, a lawyer must continue representation of a client:
    a. unless the client's cause sincerely offends the lawyer.
    b. notwithstanding good cause for terminating the representation.
    c. but not if the client refuses to pay for the lawyer's services.
    d. only if the client posts a bond to pay for the court-ordered services.

10. A client can terminate the lawyer-client relationship at any time, but the lawyer may be entitled to:
    a. quasi-contract damages or compensation for services rendered, and the client's position must not be jeopardized.
    b. full compensation for the agreed upon contract amount or the balance of the

retainer if the client unjustifiably breached the employment contract.

   c. nothing because the lawyer failed to bring the client's case to a close.

   d. a fair and reasonable compensation package as determined by the court.

11. After being discharged by a client, a lawyer has duty to:

   a. take reasonable steps to protect the client's interest, including turning over files to the client to aid in continued representation and returning the balance of any retainer.

   b. have no further contact with the client to avoid any potential conflict of interest with a new lawyer.

   c. take reasonable steps to collect all past due fees which will enable the lawyer to close the file and not sue the client thereby hindering the client's legal position.

   d. notify all potential adverse parties that the lawyer no longer represents the client and that the lawyer is available for representation, barring any conflict of interest.

12. A client may be able to avoid a lawyer-client contract if:

   a. the client can show the lawyer's conduct and performance were beneath the standard of a reasonable lawyer under the same or similar circumstances.

   b. a reasonable person would interpret the contract as fair and reasonable but for the lawyer's failing to disclose its terms and conditions.

   c. it is formed after the lawyer has finished providing services and the client was not informed of the facts needed to evaluate the appropriateness of the lawyer's compensation or benefits through the contract.

   d. a judicial representative tells the client that the contract can be avoided.

13. A lawyer and client can agree to limit the lawyer's duties if the client is:

   a. provided with a written list of limited services the lawyer will and will not provide.

   b. adequately informed and consents to the limitation, and the terms of the limitation are reasonable in the circumstances.

   c. a prepaid legal services client and the limited duties are previously set forth in the prepaid legal services contract.

   d. paying only a fee-for-services basis, and the list of available services is limited in writing.

14. A lawyer cannot charge a client a fee:

   a. if the client cannot afford any legal representation because the rules mandate attorneys provide such clients pro bono representation upon presentation.

   b. if the client declares bankruptcy after the initiation of the legal representation.

   c. if there is no written fee agreement as required under the Statute of Frauds.

   d. without the client's agreement to do so.

15. Contingency fees are permissible:

   a. if the fee agreement is in writing, is signed by the client, and includes the percentages earned by the lawyer under all circumstances and whether expenses are deducted before or after the contingent fee is calculated.

b. only in personal injury cases when the lawyer for the injured party has executed lien agreements with medical and related service providers who are thereby guaranteed payment prior to the lawyer's contingency fee.

c. when the lawyer and client have engaged in an arm's length negotiation over the contingency fees which are set forth in a clear writing understandable by a non-lawyer.

d. in divorce cases only if both parties to the divorce agree to them and the amount is limited to avoid unjust hardship on either party.

16. Fee splitting between lawyer in different firms is permitted if:

a. the court approves the fees after conclusion of the case and considers the nature and scope of each attorney's representation.

b. the client has previously waived any conflict of interest by the lawyers in both firms.

c. the client has contracted in writing with both lawyers and allocated the percentage of fees to each based upon a reasonable assessment of each attorney's satisfactory performance in the matter.

d. division is in proportion to services performed by each lawyer or each lawyer assumes joint liability for representation, the client agrees to the arrangement in writing, and the total fee is reasonable.

17. The Rules of Professional Responsibility require a lawyer to:

a. procrastinate in representation if it would be in the client's best interest.

b. consult with a client about the status of the case only when doing so is in the client's best interest.

c. reveal confidential matters to others the attorney reasonably believes can assist in achieving the client's objectives.

d. effectively represent the client with diligence and care which involves timely representation, keeping the client informed about the case, and consulting with the client on objectives.

18. A lawyer may take actions on the client's behalf:

a. only as authorized by the client through the lawyer-client contractual agreement.

b. if the lawyer knows the client would not object to the actions.

c. as they are implicitly authorized to carry out the representation, particularly with respect to technical, legal, and tactical strategy matters.

d. only if in possession of a signed retainer agreement and payment.

REGULATION OF THE LEGAL PROFESSION

ANSWERS TO REVIEW QUESTIONS

Answer 1

The correct answer is choice C. A lawyer, when appointed by a criminal court to represent a client, may refuse to represent the client for good cause shown if representation would violate the Rules of Professional Conduct or the law, or cause the lawyer undue financial burden, or the client or the cause is so repugnant to the lawyer as to likely impair the lawyer-client relationship or representation of the client.

Answer 2

The correct answer is choice D. A lawyer should reject representation of a client if the client's position is legally baseless. Further, a lawyer should reject representation of a client if the lawyer lacks the legal competence to handle the client's case, or if the client asks a lawyer to counsel on committing a criminal act.

Answer 3

The correct answer is choice B. The client possesses the ultimate authority to determine the objectives of any legal representation by a lawyer.

Answer 4

The correct answer is choice B. If the client is charged with a violation of criminal law, the lawyer must abide by the client's decision regarding whether the client will testify and whether the client will waive a jury trial.

Answer 5

The correct answer is choice A. When representing a client with diminished capacity, a lawyer may take reasonably necessary protective action and is implicitly authorized to reveal information about the client but only to the extent reasonably necessary to protect the client's interest.

Answer 6

The correct answer is choice B. When a lawyer discusses with a client a course of criminal conduct being contemplated by the client, the lawyer may discuss the nature and ramifications of the proposed criminal conduct.

Answer 7

The correct answer is choice B. A lawyer must withdraw or decline representation of a client if the lawyer's physical or mental condition impairs representation. Further, a lawyer must withdraw or decline representation of a client if the representation violates the law or the Rules of Professional Conduct, or the client discharges the lawyer.

Answer 8

The correct answer is choice A. A lawyer may withdraw from representing a client if good cause for withdrawal exists or even if good cause does not exist but the lawyer's withdraw from representation has no material adverse effect on the client's interest.

Answer 9

The correct answer is choice B. If ordered by a court, the lawyer must continue to represent a client notwithstanding good cause for terminating the representation.

Answer 10

The correct answer is choice A. A client can terminate the lawyer-client relationship at any time, but the lawyer may be entitled to quasi-contract damages or compensation for services rendered, and the client's position must not be jeopardized by the termination of legal services.

Answer 11

The correct answer is choice A. A lawyer who is discharged by a client must take reasonable steps to protect the client's interest, including turning over files to the client to aid in continued representation and returning the balance of any retainer.

Answer 12

The correct answer is choice C. A client may be able to avoid a lawyer-client contract if it is formed after the lawyer has finished providing services and the client was not informed of the facts needed to evaluate the appropriateness of the lawyer's compensation or benefits through the contract.

Answer 13

The correct answer is choice B. A lawyer's duties may be limited if the lawyer and client agree to limitations, and the client is adequately informed and consents to the limitations, and the terms of the limitation are reasonable in the circumstances.

Answer 14

The correct answer is choice D. A lawyer cannot charge a client a fee without the client's agreement to do so. The rules include provisions concerning what amounts to a reasonable fee agreement, including payments for services rendered that take into account services expected, the skills of the lawyer, the nature and difficulty of the case, and the reasonableness of expenses.

Answer 15

The correct answer is choice A. Contingency fees are permissible if the fee agreement is in writing, is signed by the client, and includes the percentages earned by the lawyer in all circumstances and whether expenses are deducted before or after the contingent fee is calculated.

Answer 16

The correct answer is choice D. Fee splitting between lawyers in different firms is permitted if division is in proportion to services performed by each lawyer or each lawyer assumes joint liability for representation, the client agrees to the arrangement in writing, and the total fee is reasonable.

Answer 17

The correct answer is choice D. The Rules of Professional Responsibility require a lawyer to exercise diligence and care in representing a client. This includes no procrastinating in representation, informing and consulting with a client about the status of the case and explaining matters to the client in a manner the client will understand and allow the client to make an informed decision regarding the representation, and reasonably consulting with the client about the means by which the objectives will be accomplished.

Answer 18

The correct answer is choice C. A lawyer may take actions on the client's behalf as they are implicitly authorized to carry out the representation, particularly with respect to technical, legal, and tactical strategy matters.

★★★★ **III.   CLIENT CONFIDENTIALITY**

The principle of client-lawyer confidentiality is given effect by related bodies of law: the attorney-client privilege, the work product doctrine, and the rule of confidentiality established in professional ethics. Model Rules of Prof'l Conduct R. 1.6 cmt. [3]. The evidentiary attorney-client privilege is based upon the Federal Rules of Evidence, and work product immunity is an exception to the evidentiary privilege under the Federal Rules of Civil Procedure. The duty of confidentiality is distinct from the evidentiary privilege in that it exists in the client-lawyer relationship and is based upon the Rules and/or the Restatement. These three concepts will be separately addressed below.

★★★   **A.   Attorney-Client Privilege**

For purposes of the MPRE, the Federal Rules of Evidence and the Federal Rules of Civil Procedure govern the scope of the attorney-client evidentiary privilege.

1)   WHEN STATE LAW OF EVIDENTIARY PRIVILEGES APPLIES

State law of evidentiary privileges usually applies in a state court that is applying state law. Generally, federal constitutional law, statutes, rules, or common law will govern privileges applied by federal courts. Fed. R. Evid. 501. An exception to this rule applies in civil cases when state law supplies the rule of decision regarding an element of a claim or defense; in that event, the evidentiary privilege must be determined based on state law. *Id.* This might occur, for example, when a federal court is sitting in diversity jurisdiction in a civil case and applying state law. In that event, an evidentiary privilege could be determined based on state law.

Although the MPRE will probably not test the foregoing principles, it is useful to know that there are different types of privileges. Those principles are relevant because they indicate that even under the Federal Rules of Evidence, the following general legal principles of evidentiary privileges can apply. Therefore, although state-specific evidentiary privileges won't be tested, it is necessary to know these general principles for the MPRE.

2)   GENERAL LAW OF EVIDENTIARY PRIVILEGES

a)   Privileged Communications

A person or an entity may communicate with a lawyer as a potential or existing client. If the communication is a casual one not conducted for the purpose of obtaining legal advice or representation, it is not considered confidential. If that communication is made to obtain legal representation or advice, it is confidential and therefore legally privileged from disclosure. That privilege exists even if the potential or existing client communicated with someone reasonably believed to be, but who in fact was not, a lawyer. The privilege applies irrespective of whether the lawyer provided any advice or representation to the person.

b)   Holder of the Privilege

Generally, a *client* holds the privilege of confidential communications with the client's lawyer. The client usually may exercise that privilege by preventing anyone from disclosing to any third party, or testifying about, the confidential communication. Generally, the privilege continues even after the death of the client or lawyer. A lawyer is obligated to assert the privilege to protect a client who cannot assert it for a valid reason, such as incapacity or death.

c) General Exceptions to the Privilege

The privilege exists unless: (1) the client waives confidentiality as to one or more issues; or (2) the client or the lawyer breaches a duty that is owed to the other.

The privilege does not apply:

- to physical evidence that the client provides to the lawyer;
- to documents preexisting the attorney-client relationship; or
- if the lawyer's services were requested to assist in planning or committing a crime or a fraud.

(1) Examples

- Not Privileged

A routine report that a company's non-attorney employee prepared for the company's executive or according to company policy does not become privileged because the company provided the report to its lawyer for the purpose of litigation.

- Privileged

If a lawyer hires a physician to examine a patient, a confidential communication from the patient to the physician, which is subsequently conveyed to the lawyer, is subject to the attorney-client privilege because the physician acted as the lawyer's agent.

B. Work Product Doctrine

Work product immunity may protect a lawyer from the requirement of disclosing to a third party some of the information that the lawyer acquired while preparing for litigation. Federal Rule of Civil Procedure 26(b)(3) provides qualified immunity, which means that work product materials are only subject to discovery if the party requesting them proves: (1) a substantial need for the materials; and (2) an inability to obtain a substantial equivalent of those materials by another method.

A lawyer will have absolute immunity from disclosing work product documents that include the lawyer's "mental impressions, conclusions, opinions, or legal theories" regarding litigation. Fed. R. Civ. P. 26(b)(3).

★★★ ## C. Professional Obligation of Confidentiality

The professional obligation of confidentiality is separate and distinct from the attorney-client evidentiary privilege. For purposes of the MPRE, the Rules and/or the Restatement govern the professional obligation of confidentiality in the client-lawyer relationship.

1) DUTIES TO PROSPECTIVE CLIENT

A person who discusses with a lawyer the possibility of forming a client-lawyer relationship with respect to a matter is a prospective client. Model Rules of Prof'l Conduct R. 1.18(a).

Even when no client-lawyer relationship ensues, a lawyer who has had discussions with a prospective client must not use or reveal information learned in the consultation, except as Rule 1.9, regarding conflict of interests, would permit with respect to a former client's information. Model Rules of Prof'l Conduct R. 1.18(b).

2) CONFIDENTIALITY OF INFORMATION

A lawyer must never reveal information relating to the representation of a client *unless*:

- the client gives informed consent;
- the disclosure is impliedly authorized in order to carry out the representation; or
- the disclosure is permitted under the Rules.

Model Rules of Prof'l Conduct R. 1.6(a).

This general Rule is referred to elsewhere in this outline as the Rule of Confidentiality. Several other Rules refer to or relate to this Rule of Confidentiality.

D. Disclosures Expressly or Impliedly Authorized by Client

1) CLIENT-AUTHORIZED DISCLOSURE

Under certain circumstances, a client can authorize disclosure of confidential information that is otherwise subject to the previously described attorney-client evidentiary privilege.

The Rule of Confidentiality provides that a lawyer can reveal information relating to the representation of a client if the client provides either informed express or implied consent. Model Rules of Prof'l Conduct R. 1.6(a).

a) Express Consent

Express consent exists after a lawyer provides the client sufficient information to enable the client to recognize the waiver's impact, and the client approves of the waiver.

b) Implied Consent

Implied consent means that, even without obtaining a client's express approval of waiving the protections of the Rule of Confidentiality, a lawyer can disclose confidential client information for the purposes of representing the client. For example, a lawyer may reveal such confidential client information in order to obtain a "satisfactory conclusion" of a matter for the client. Model Rules of Prof'l Conduct R. 1.6 cmt. [5].

★★ **E.** **Other Exceptions to the Confidentiality Rule**

A lawyer may disclose confidential information under certain additional circumstances. Particularly, a lawyer may reveal information relating to the representation of a client to the extent the lawyer reasonably believes necessary:

- to prevent reasonably certain death or substantial bodily harm;
- to prevent the client from committing a crime or fraud that is reasonably certain to result in substantial injury to the financial interests or property of another and in furtherance of which the client has used or is using the lawyer's services;
- to prevent, mitigate, or rectify substantial injury to the financial interests or property of another that is reasonably certain to result, or has resulted, from the client's commission of a crime or fraud, in furtherance of which the client has used the lawyer's services;
- to secure legal advice about the lawyer's compliance with the Rules;
- to establish a claim or defense in a dispute between the lawyer and the client;
- to establish a defense to a criminal charge or civil claim against the lawyer based on conduct in which the client was involved,
- to respond to allegations in any proceeding concerning the lawyer's representation of the client;
- to comply with other law or a court order; or
- to detect and resolve conflicts of interest arising from the lawyer's change of employment or from changes in the composition or ownership of a firm, but only if the revealed information would not compromise the attorney-client privilege or otherwise prejudice the client.

Model Rules of Prof'l Conduct R. 1.6(b).

CLIENT CONFIDENTIALITY

REVIEW QUESTIONS

1. Communications made between a client or potential client and a lawyer are:
   a. confidential, except if the lawyer has a conflict of interest with a pre-existing client and must disclose the visit and communications by the potential client to the pre-existing client.
   b. confidential and legally privileged from disclosure, regardless of whether the lawyer provides advice or representation.
   c. confidential, except to the extent that the confidential communication is previously known to the lawyer, and the lawyer advises the potential client that the lawyer already knew the information.
   d. not confidential because without a representation agreement, no attorney-client relationship is established.

2. The privilege of confidential communication does not apply when:
   a. the client waives confidentiality as to any issue or the client or lawyer breaches a duty owed to the other.
   b. the client provides a written confession of a crime to a lawyer.
   c. the lawyer is representing a client who has previously been convicted of perjury.
   d. the lawyer is fired by the client who refused to pay for services rendered.

3. Attorney work-product immunity protects lawyers from disclosing some information acquired or created during preparation for litigation. Qualified immunity extends to work product materials. However, otherwise protected materials are discoverable if the party seeking discovery shows:
   a. manifest injustice would occur if the immunity were allowed to stand and the party seeking the material was denied access to it.
   b. both substantial need for the material and inability to obtain the substantial equivalent of the materials by another method.
   c. the work product was developed for the purpose of obtaining an unfair advantage at trial.
   d. a clear and present danger that without such information the party will suffer irreparable harm.

4. A lawyer has absolute immunity for disclosing work-product as to the lawyer's:
   a. mental impressions, conclusions, opinions, or legal theories regarding litigation.
   b. calculations concerning damages to be sought from the opposing party.
   c. adverse witness list.
   d. fees charged to the client.

5. A lawyer owes a professional obligation of confidentiality to a prospective client and cannot reveal information relating to possible representation of the client:

a. unless the client reveals the information to the lawyer to prevent discovery of a crime or fraud.
b. without the client's explicit or implicit consent or unless otherwise consistent with the Rules.
c. except if the lawyer clearly informs the client, in writing and prior to any client statement, that confidentiality attaches upon engagement of the attorney.
d. if the client explicitly or implicitly retains the lawyer.

CLIENT CONFIDENTIALITY

ANSWERS TO REVIEW QUESTIONS

Answer 1

The correct answer is choice B. Communications made between a client or potential client and a lawyer are confidential and, therefore, legally privileged from disclosure, regardless of whether the lawyer provides advice or representation.

Answer 2

The correct answer is choice A. The privilege of confidential communication does not apply if the client waives confidentiality as to any issue or the client or lawyer breaches a duty owed to the other. Further, the privilege does not apply to physical evidence supplied by the client to the lawyer, to documents preexisting the attorney-client relationship, or if the lawyer's services were requested to assist in planning or committing a crime or a fraud.

Answer 3

The correct answer is choice B. Qualified immunity extends to work product materials, but they are discoverable if the party seeking discovery shows both substantial need for the material and inability to obtain the substantial equivalent of the material by another method.

Answer 4

The correct answer is choice A. A lawyer has absolute immunity for disclosing work-product as to the lawyer's mental impressions, conclusions, opinions, or legal theories regarding litigation.

Answer 5

The correct answer is choice B. A lawyer owes a professional obligation of confidentiality to a prospective client and cannot reveal information relating to possible representation of the client without the client's explicit or implicit consent or unless otherwise consistent with the Rules.

IV.   CONFLICTS OF INTEREST

A practicing lawyer often encounters conflicting responsibilities. Many ethical problems arise from a conflict between a lawyer's responsibilities to clients, to the legal system, and to the lawyer's own interest. The Rules often provide guidelines for resolving these conflicts.

A.   Current Client Conflicts – Multiple Clients and Joint Representation

1)   MULTIPLE CLIENTS

a)   General Rule--Client 1 v. Client 2

Generally, a lawyer cannot represent a client if the representation involves a concurrent conflict of interest. Model Rules of Prof'l Conduct R. 1.7(a). A concurrent conflict of interest exists if: (1) the representation of one client will be directly adverse to another client; or (2) there is a significant risk that the representation of one or more clients will be materially limited by the lawyer's responsibilities to another client, a former client, a third person, or by the lawyer's personal interest. *Id.*

(1)   Exceptions

The lawyer may, however, engage in representation involving a concurrent conflict of interest if:

- the lawyer reasonably believes that the lawyer will be able to provide competent and diligent representation to each affected client;
- the representation is not prohibited by law;
- the representation does not involve the assertion of a claim by one client against another client represented by the lawyer in the same litigation or other proceeding before a tribunal; and
- each affected client gives informed consent, in writing, to this representation.

Model Rules of Prof'l Conduct R. 1.7(b).

2)   JOINT REPRESENTATION

When a lawyer represents multiple clients in a single matter, the consultation must include an explanation of the common representation and the risks involved. Model Rules of Prof'l Conduct R. 1.7 cmt. [18]. Special considerations exist, however, when representing criminal defendants. Generally, a lawyer should decline to represent more than one criminal co-defendant. Model Rules of Prof'l Conduct R. 1.7 cmt. [23].

a)   Aggregate Settlement

A lawyer who represents two or more co-clients must not participate: (1) in making an aggregate settlement of the civil claims of or against the clients; or (2) in a criminal case, an aggregated agreement as to guilty or *nolo contendere* pleas, unless each client gives informed consent in a writing signed by the client. Model Rules of Prof'l Conduct R. 1.8(g). The lawyer's disclosure must include the existence and nature of all the claims or pleas involved and of the participation of each person in the settlement. *Id.*

B. Current Client Conflicts - Lawyer's Personal Interest or Duties

A lawyer whose personal interest might negatively impact the lawyer's relationship with a potential client may decline representation of the potential client. Model Rules of Prof'l Conduct R. 1.7. For example, a lawyer may decline representing a potential client who seeks to bring a civil action against a childhood friend of the lawyer. The relationship with the childhood friend may adversely affect the lawyer's ability to provide detached representation.

C. Former Client Conflicts

★★★   1)   DUTIES TO FORMER CLIENTS

a)   General Rule--Client v. Former Client

A lawyer who represented a client in a matter must not later represent another person in the same or a substantially related matter in which that person's interests are materially adverse to the interests of the former client, unless the former client gives informed written consent. Model Rules of Prof'l Conduct R. 1.9(a).

b)   Former Firm

A lawyer must not knowingly represent a person in the same or a substantially related matter in which a firm that the lawyer was formerly associated with had previously represented a client: (1) whose interests are materially adverse to that person; and (2) about whom the lawyer had acquired information protected by the Rule of Confidentiality and Rule 1.9(c), discussed below, that is material to the matter, unless the former client gives informed written consent. Rules of Prof'l Conduct R. 1.9(b).

c)   Use of Former Client's Information

A lawyer who represented a client in a matter, or whose present or former firm represented a client in a matter, must not later (1) use information relating to the representation to the disadvantage of the former client or (2) reveal information relating to the representation except as the Rules would permit or require or when the information has become generally known. Model Rules of Prof'l Conduct R. 1.9(c).

      d)   Former and Current Government Officers and Employees

A lawyer who served as a public officer or government employee is subject to Rule 1.9(c) discussed above regarding a lawyer's duties with respect to a former client's information. Model Rules of Prof'l Conduct R. 1.11(a). Additionally, a lawyer who served as a public officer or government employee must not represent a client in connection with a matter in which the lawyer participated personally and substantially unless the appropriate government agency gives its informed written consent to the representation. *Id.*

D.   Prospective Client Conflicts

A lawyer may encounter a situation in which a prospective client made confidential communications, and then later a person with materially adverse interests seeks the lawyer's representation in the matter. The lawyer cannot represent the second person under these circumstances. In particular, a lawyer cannot represent a client with interests materially adverse to those of a prospective client in the same or a substantially related matter if the lawyer received information from the prospective client that could be significantly harmful to the person in the matter. Model Rules of Prof'l Conduct R. 1.18(c). This provision is subject to the following exception.

When the lawyer has received disqualifying information under the circumstances in the preceding paragraph, the lawyer may represent the client if:

- Both the affected client and the prospective client give their informed written consent; or
- In the situation of a law firm, the lawyer who received the information took reasonable measures to avoid exposure to more disqualifying information than was reasonably necessary to determine whether to represent the prospective client; and
  - The disqualified lawyer is timely screened from any participation in the matter and is apportioned no part of the fee from the matter; and
  - Written notice is promptly given to the prospective client.

Model Rules of Prof'l Conduct R. 1.18(d).

E.   Imputed Conflicts

When two lawyers have a special relationship, the conflicts of one lawyer may be ascribed to the other lawyer.

★★   1)   LAWYERS ASSOCIATED IN A FIRM

While lawyers are associated in a firm, none of them can knowingly represent a client when any one of them practicing alone would be prohibited from doing so because of a conflict of interest. Model Rules of Prof'l Conduct R. 1.10(a). The conflict of one lawyer in the firm is *imputed* to all lawyers in the firm.

        a)   Exceptions

There are two exceptions when a conflict of one lawyer in a firm will not be imputed to another lawyer in the firm.

(1)   No Significant Risk of Limiting Representation

A conflict of one lawyer in a firm is not imputed to other lawyers in the firm when the disqualified lawyer's prohibition is based on a personal interest and would not present a significant risk of materially limiting the representation of the client by the firm's remaining lawyers. *Id.*

★★   (2)   Screening

A conflict of one lawyer in a firm is not imputed to other lawyers in the firm when the prohibition arises out of the disqualified lawyer's association with a prior firm and the disqualified lawyer is adequately screened from the case as follows:

- The disqualified lawyer must be timely screened from any participation in the matter and be apportioned no part of the fee from it; and
- Written notice must promptly be provided to any affected former client. The notice must include: a description of the screening procedures employed; a statement of the firm's and the screened lawyer's compliance with these Rules; a statement that review may be available before a tribunal; and an agreement by the firm to respond promptly to any written inquiries or objections by the former client about the screening procedures; and
- Certifications of compliance with the screening requirements and procedures must be provided to the former client by the screened lawyer and by a partner of the firm at reasonable intervals, upon the former client's written request, and upon termination of the screening procedures. *Id.*

2)   LAWYER DISSOCIATED FROM A FIRM

When a lawyer has terminated an association with a firm, the firm is not prohibited from representing a person with interests materially adverse to those of a client represented by the formerly associated lawyer and not currently represented by the firm, unless: (1) the matter is the same or substantially related to that in which the formerly associated lawyer represented the client; and (2) any lawyer remaining in the firm has information protected by the Rule of Confidentiality and Rule 1.9(c), regarding a lawyer's duties with respect to a former client's information, that is material to the matter. Model Rules of Prof'l Conduct R. 1.10(b).

3)   WAIVER

An imputed conflict of interest may be waived by the affected client's informed written consent. Model Rules of Prof'l Conduct R. 1.10(c).

★   **F.   Acquiring an Interest in Litigation**

A lawyer cannot acquire a proprietary interest in a cause of action or subject matter of litigation that the lawyer is conducting for a client. Model Rules of Prof'l Conduct R. 1.8(i). The lawyer may, however: (1) acquire a lien authorized by law to secure the lawyer's fee or expenses; and (2) contract with a client for a reasonable contingent fee in a civil case. *Id.*

★ **G.   Business Transactions with Client**

1)   LIMITATIONS ON BUSINESS TRANSACTIONS WITH CLIENT

Generally, a lawyer may pursue a business transaction with, or adverse to, a client only under limited circumstances. Specifically, a lawyer cannot enter into such a transaction or knowingly acquire an ownership, possessory, security, or other pecuniary interest adverse to a client *unless*:

- The transaction is fair and reasonable to the client, fully disclosed in writing to the client in a manner that can be reasonably understood; and
- The client is advised in writing of the desirability of seeking independent counsel and is given a reasonable opportunity to do so; and
- The client provides informed written consent to the transaction and the lawyer's role in the transaction, including whether the lawyer is representing the client in the transaction.

Model Rules of Prof'l Conduct R. 1.8(a).

2)   USE OF CLIENT'S INFORMATION

A lawyer must not use information relating to representation of a client to the client's disadvantage unless the client gives informed consent, except as permitted or required by these Rules. Model Rules of Prof'l Conduct R. 1.8(b).

★★ 3)   LIMITATION ON GIFTS

A lawyer must not solicit any substantial gift from a client, including a testamentary gift, or prepare on behalf of a client an instrument giving the lawyer or a person related to the lawyer any substantial gift, unless the lawyer or other recipient of the gift is related to the client. Model Rules of Prof'l Conduct R. 1.8(c). Related persons include a spouse, child, grandchild, parent, grandparent, or other relative or individual with whom the lawyer or the client maintains a close familial relationship. *Id.*

4)   MEDIA OR LITERARY RIGHTS

Prior to the conclusion of representation of a client, a lawyer cannot make or negotiate an agreement giving the lawyer literary or media rights to a portrayal or account based in substantial part on information relating to the representation. Model Rules of Prof'l Conduct R. 1.8(d).

★★ 5)   FINANCIAL ASSISTANCE TO CLIENT

A lawyer must not provide financial assistance to a client in connection with pending or contemplated litigation, *except* that a lawyer may advance court costs and expenses of litigation, the payment of which may be contingent upon the outcome of the matter; and a lawyer representing an indigent client may pay court costs and expenses of litigation on behalf of the client. Model Rules of Prof'l Conduct R. 1.8(e).

★

6) SEXUAL RELATIONS WITH CLIENT

As a general principle, a lawyer may not coerce, intimidate, or take advantage of any client in an attempt to have sexual relations. This rule is intended to prohibit sexual exploitation by a lawyer in the course of professional representation.

Specifically, a lawyer must not have sexual relations with a client unless a consensual sexual relationship existed between them when the client-lawyer relationship commenced. Model Rules of Prof'l Conduct R. 1.8(j).

★

H. Third-Party Compensation and Influence

In practice, a third party might pay for a lawyer to represent a client, which may create a conflict of interest if the third party's interests in the representation are not the same as the client's. A lawyer cannot accept compensation from someone other than the client unless:

- The client gives informed consent;
- There is no interference with the lawyer's independence of professional judgment or with the client-lawyer relationship; and
- The information relating to representation of a client is protected as required by the Rule of Confidentiality.

Model Rules of Prof'l Conduct R. 1.8(f).

★

I. Lawyers Currently or Formerly in Government Service

The disqualification of lawyers associated in a firm with former or current government lawyers is governed by Rule 1.11 discussed above. Model Rules of Prof'l Conduct R. 1.10(d).

When a lawyer who served as a public officer or employee of the government is disqualified from representation, no lawyer in a firm with which that lawyer is associated may knowingly undertake or continue representation in such a matter unless: (1) the disqualified lawyer is timely screened from any participation in the matter and is apportioned no part of the fee; and (2) written notice is promptly given to the appropriate government agency to enable it to ascertain compliance with these provisions. Model Rules of Prof'l Conduct R. 1.11(b).

J. Former Judge. Arbitrator, Mediator, or Other Third-Party Neutral

Generally, a lawyer must not represent anyone in connection with a matter in which the lawyer participated personally and substantially: (1) as a judge or other adjudicative officer, or law clerk to such a person, or 2) as an arbitrator, mediator, or other third-party neutral, *unless* all parties to the proceeding give informed written consent. Model Rules of Prof'l Conduct R. 1.12(a).

CONFLICTS OF INTEREST

REVIEW QUESTIONS

1. A lawyer can enter into a business transaction with a client under limited circumstances if:
   a. both the lawyer and the client seek independent counsel with regard to the proposed business transaction and are both advised that it does not present a conflict of interest.
   b. the transaction is fair and reasonable to the client and fully disclosed in writing, and the client is advised in writing of the desirability of seeking independent counsel and is given an opportunity to do so, and the client agrees in writing to the transaction.
   c. the client waives, in writing, any possible conflict of interest to the extent that it might impede either the business transaction or the lawyer's ability to demonstrate independent judgment.
   d. the lawyer agrees to not represent the client in any future matters including those related to the business transaction.

2. A lawyer cannot receive or solicit any gift from a client:
   a. unless the lawyer is related to the client or has a close family relationship with the client.
   b. unless the gift is trivial, a token, or otherwise has no value.
   c. unless the lawyer is romantically involved with the client.
   d. unless the gift is received from a client's trust and the client has no control over the trust.

3. A lawyer cannot make or negotiate literary or media rights to a portrayal of the representation of a client:
   a. except if the client agrees in writing and is represented by independent counsel in negotiations of the rights with the lawyer.
   b. under any circumstances.
   c. unless the client receives preferential rights.
   d. except if the client is placed in the most favorable light possible in the portrayal.

4. A lawyer cannot provide financial assistance to a client related to pending or contemplated litigation:
   a. except for court costs and expenses which may be advanced contingent on the outcome of a matter, or court costs and expenses for an indigent client.
   b. unless the client's assets are currently unavailable and the lawyer is assigned an interest in the assets plus reasonable interest for the time period the lawyer advances funds.
   c. except if the client is a minor and has attachable assets available to pay the

attorney upon reaching majority.

    d. except for advances on an estate in probate if the estate has guaranteed all legal fees related to the probate.

5. A lawyer may not have sexual relations with a client during the course of representation:
    a. unless the sexual relationship is consensual.
    b. unless the sexual relationship existed without any instigation by the lawyer.
    c. unless the sexual relationship existed when the client/lawyer relationship commenced.
    d. under any circumstances.

6. A lawyer's representation of two clients simultaneously presents a conflict of interest when:
    a. both clients object to the lawyer's actions in representing the other client.
    b. one client objects to the lawyer's actions in representing the other client.
    c. the interests of the clients are directly adverse.
    d. the lawyer perceives a possible conflict.

7. Generally, a lawyer should not represent more than one codefendant in a criminal matter. However, if a lawyer does undertake joint representation of criminal defendants:
    a. the lawyer cannot participate in making an aggregate agreement for guilty or no contest pleas unless each client signs informed consents that explain each client's participation in the agreement.
    b. the lawyer must inform the court prior to entering the pleas so that the judge can advise each client to retain separate counsel and avoid a conflict of interest.
    c. each codefendant is entitled to know the complete terms and conditions of any plea agreement reached by the other codefendant prior to entering their plea.
    d. the lawyer must prorate legal fees so as not to charge either of the codefendants more than the other.

8. A lawyer has a conflict of interest when:
    a. continued representation of a client will adversely impact the lawyer's ability to attract more clients.
    b. there is a significant risk that representation of one or more clients will be materially limited by the lawyer's previously scheduled personal matters.
    c. a lawyer believes a client is lying beyond a reasonable doubt and the lies impede the lawyer's ability to represent the client with a clear conscience.
    d. One client's interest is directly adverse to another client's interest or there is a significant risk that representation of a client will be limited by responsibilities to another client.

9. A lawyer cannot represent a new client in the same or a substantially related matter relating to a former client if that new client's interests are materially adverse to the interests of the former client unless:
    a. the former client gives written informed consent.
    b. both the former and current client give written informed consent.

c. the lawyer obtains signed, written waivers of confidentiality from both clients.

d. the former client gives verbal informed consent.

10. When a lawyer who formerly served as a government agency employee or officer is disqualified from representation of a client:

    a. the lawyer and any member of the lawyer's firm can represent the client if there is written informed consent given by the client to the firm and the lawyer's former government employer.

    b. no lawyer in the lawyer's firm can be involved in the representation unless the disqualified lawyer is screened from any representation in the matter, gets no fee from the matter, and notice is given to the former government agency of the representation.

    c. the lawyer's firm is wholly disqualified from representing the client.

    d. the government agency that formerly employed the lawyer can release the lawyer, in writing, from any conflict of interest.

11. If a lawyer wants to represent a client but previously served as an arbitrator, mediator, or judge in a matter in which the client was once involved, there is a conflict of interest and the lawyer cannot represent the client unless:

    a. all parties involved in the matter give informed consent in writing to the representation.

    b. the lawyer and the lawyer's firm agree to never represent an interest adverse to any of the parties involved in the matter.

    c. a neutral magistrate reviews the matter and, after all parties are given an opportunity to be heard on the matter, holds that the lawyer may represent the client.

    d. there is a written offer, acceptance, and consideration between the parties waiving the conflict.

CONFLICTS OF INTEREST

ANSWERS TO REVIEW QUESTIONS

Answer 1

The correct answer is choice B. A lawyer can enter into a business transaction with a client under limited circumstances if the transaction is fair and reasonable to the client and fully disclosed in writing, and the client is advised in writing of the desirability of seeking independent counsel and is given an opportunity to do so, and the client agrees in writing to the transaction.

Answer 2

The correct answer is choice A. A lawyer cannot receive or solicit any gift from a client unless the lawyer is related to the client or unless the lawyer has a close family relationship with the client.

Answer 3

The correct answer is choice B. Prior to the conclusion of representation of a client, a lawyer cannot make or negotiate literary or media rights to a portrayal of the representation of a client.

Answer 4

The correct answer is choice A. A lawyer cannot provide financial assistance to a client related to pending or contemplated litigation except for court costs and expenses which may be advanced contingent on outcome of the matter or to pay court costs and expenses for an indigent client.

Answer 5

The correct answer is choice C. A lawyer may not have sexual relations with a client during the course of representation unless the sexual relationship existed when the client/lawyer relationship commenced.

Answer 6

The correct answer is choice C. A lawyer's representation of two clients simultaneously presents a conflict of interest if the interests of the clients are directly adverse.

Answer 7

The correct answer is choice A. Generally, a lawyer should not represent more than one codefendant in a criminal matter. However, if the lawyer does represent more than one criminal codefendant, the lawyer cannot participate in making an aggregate agreement for guilty or no contest pleas unless each client signs informed consents that explain each client's participation in the agreement.

Answer 8

The correct answer is choice D. A lawyer has a conflict of interest if representation of one client is directly adverse to another client's interest, or there is a significant risk that representation of one or more clients will be materially limited by the lawyer's responsibilities to another party, person, or the lawyer's own interest. An exception exists if the lawyer reasonably believes the lawyer will be able to provide competent representation to each affected client, the representation is not prohibited by law, the representation does not involve assertion of a direct claim by one client against another client, and each affected client provides informed written agreement to representation.

Answer 9

The correct answer is choice A. A lawyer cannot represent a new client in the same or a substantially related matter relating to a former client if that new client's interests are materially adverse to the interests of the former client unless the former client gives written informed consent.

Answer 10

The correct answer is choice B. If a lawyer who formerly served as a government agency employee or officer is disqualified from representation of a client, no lawyer in the lawyer's firm can be involved in the representation unless the disqualified lawyer is screened from any representation in the matter, gets no fee from the matter, and notice is given to the former government agency of the representation.

Answer 11

The correct answer is choice A. If a lawyer wants to represent a client but previously served as an arbitrator, mediator, or judge in a matter in which the client was once involved, there is a conflict of interest and the lawyer cannot represent the client unless all parties involved in the matter give informed consent in writing to the representation.

V. COMPETENCE, MALPRACTICE, AND OTHER CIVIL LIABILITY

★★   **A. Maintaining Competence**

1) DUTY OF COMPETENCE

A lawyer has a duty to act competently with regard to legal representation. Generally, a lawyer must apply the 1) diligence, 2) learning and skill, and 3) mental, emotional, and physical ability reasonably necessary for the performance of the legal service requested.

2) OBLIGATION TO MAINTAIN COMPETENCE

A lawyer has an obligation to not only have the competence to handle a matter, but also to maintain competence through ongoing learning or continuing legal education and keeping abreast of ongoing changes in the law. In some jurisdictions, such study and education is voluntary. In other jurisdictions, the professional authority makes such study and education mandatory.

The duty to maintain competence also includes keeping informed of the benefits and risks associated with relevant technology. For example, a lawyer may be required to protect confidential electronic client information in a commercially reasonable manner.

★★   **B. Competence Necessary to Undertake Representation**

1) COMPETENCE REQUIREMENT

A lawyer must provide competent representation to a client. Model Rules of Prof'l Conduct R. 1.1. Competent representation requires the legal knowledge, skill, thoroughness, and preparation reasonably necessary for the representation. *Id.* Accordingly, a lawyer should only accept employment from a client if the lawyer has the ability to competently handle the client's matter, or can, through reasonable preparation, gain the necessary competence to handle the matter.

If a lawyer were to represent a client without being competent to do so, this could jeopardize both the client's matter and the lawyer's professional status (potential Rules violations and/or malpractice).

2) GAINING COMPETENCE

A lawyer who lacks competence in a matter can become competent by learning and preparing to practice the type of law involved. This effort should be reasonable so that it does not impose unreasonable cost and delay upon a client. A lawyer may consider whether "it is feasible to refer the matter to, or associate or consult with, a lawyer of established competence." Model Rules of Prof'l Conduct R. 1.1 cmt. [1]. For example, a lawyer can gain competence by working with another lawyer in the same firm who is competent with respect to the matter. Similarly, with a client's consent, a lawyer can gain competence by working with another lawyer who is not in the same firm as the lawyer.

★

a) Emergency Situations

In an emergency, however, a lawyer may give advice or assistance in a matter in which the lawyer does not ordinarily possess the relevant legal skill (i.e., competence). This can occur when "referral to or consultation or association with another lawyer would be impractical." Model Rules of Prof'l Conduct R. 1.1 cmt. [3]. This situation might arise, for example, when a dying person wants to make a will and does not have time to find a probate lawyer. In that event, a lawyer should limit the assistance to what is "reasonably necessary in the circumstances" to avoid placing a client's interest at risk. *Id.*

★★

C. Exercise of Diligence and Care

A lawyer must act with reasonable diligence and promptness in representing a client. Model Rules of Prof'l Conduct R. 1.3. Common exam questions involve lawyers procrastinating in different aspects of their practice. As previously mentioned, a lack of diligence can give rise to disciplinary action or civil liability.

D. Civil Liability to Client Including Malpractice

★★

1) GENERAL CONSIDERATIONS

Some attorney professional misconduct may result in disciplinary proceedings, as well as potential civil liability. For example, a lawyer's failure to timely file a pleading within the controlling statute of limitations that results in a client's loss of a cause of action violates the Rule regarding diligence and also could give rise to a civil legal malpractice action.

a) Enforcement Proceedings

An alleged violation of the Rules must be reported to the relevant professional authority, which has the authority to bring an enforcement proceeding against a lawyer. A lawyer admitted to practice in a jurisdiction is subject to the disciplinary authority of the jurisdiction, regardless of where the lawyer's conduct occurs. Model Rules of Prof'l Conduct R. 8.5(a). A lawyer not admitted to practice law in a jurisdiction is subject to the disciplinary authority of the jurisdiction if the lawyer provides or offers to provide any legal services in the jurisdiction. *Id.* A lawyer can be subject to the disciplinary authority of multiple jurisdictions for the same conduct. *Id.*

The enforcement proceeding should satisfy constitutional due process requirements to the extent that its outcome could adversely affect the lawyer's property interest in the license to practice law.

b) Civil Liability

Civil liability for violating the Rules includes tort liability for a legal malpractice cause of action and civil liability for a contract law cause of action. For example, a lawyer whose conduct violated the Rules regarding competence in handling a client's matter might also have violated a representation agreement with the client, which might support a breach of contract claim.

(1)   Legal Malpractice

Some states have codified a legal malpractice claim, which is a negligence tort claim with common law origins. Generally, a lawyer's violation of the Rules involving some actionable negligence can support a malpractice action. Usually, in addition to establishing the negligence elements of duty, breach, causation, and damages, a client must also prove that the client would have prevailed in the underlying cause of action that was adversely affected by the lawyer's professional misconduct.

E.   Civil Liability to Non-Clients

1)   GENERAL DUTY

A lawyer's duty to a client does not completely outweigh the duty to not injure a nonclient. With a few exceptions, a lawyer is subject to liability to a client or nonclient when a nonlawyer would be liable in similar circumstances. Restatement (Third) of The Law Governing Lawyers § 56. Thus, if a lawyer aids the client in the commission of a tort on a nonclient, the client-lawyer relationship would not provide a shield from liability. A lawyer has some defenses and exceptions to liability to nonclient claims if the lawyer acts merely as an advocate of a client:

- A lawyer has an absolute privilege to publish matters concerning a nonclient if: 1) the publication occurs in communications prior to or during a proceeding before a tribunal; 2) the lawyer participates as counsel in that proceeding; and 3) the matter is published to a person who may be involved in the proceeding, and the publication has some relation to the proceeding;

- A lawyer representing a client in a civil proceeding or procuring criminal proceedings by a client is not liable to a nonclient for wrongful use of civil proceedings or for malicious prosecution if the lawyer has probable cause for acting, or if the lawyer acts primarily to help the client obtain proper adjudication of the client's claim in that proceeding; and

- A lawyer who advises or assists a client to make or break a contract or to enter or dissolve a legal relationship is not liable to a nonclient for interference with a contract or a legal relationship if the lawyer acts to advance the client's interests without using wrongful means. *Id.* § 57.

2)   SPECIFIC DUTY

A lawyer owes a duty to use care to a nonclient when and to the extent that:

- The lawyer or a client invites the nonclient to rely on the lawyer's opinion or legal services, the nonclient does so rely, and the nonclient is not too remote from the lawyer to be entitled to protection;

- The lawyer knows that a client intends to primarily benefit a nonclient by the lawyer's services; that such duty would not significantly impair the lawyer's performance of obligations to the client; and the absence of such duty would make enforcement of those obligations to the client unlikely; and
- The lawyer's client is a trustee, guardian, executor, or fiduciary acting primarily to perform similar functions for the nonclient; the lawyer knows that appropriate action is necessary to prevent or rectify the breach of fiduciary duty owed by the client to the nonclient where the breach is a crime or fraud, or the lawyer assisted in the breach; the nonclient is not reasonably able to protect its rights; and such duty would not significantly impair the performance of the lawyer's obligations to the client. *Id.* § 51.

★★ **F.** **Limiting Liability for Malpractice**

A lawyer may not attempt to contract with the client to limit potential malpractice liability. Additionally, a lawyer cannot attempt to settle a claim with a client for malpractice liability unless the client is informed, in writing, of the ability to obtain independent counsel.

A lawyer must not make an agreement prospectively limiting the lawyer's liability to a client for malpractice unless the client is independently represented in making the agreement.

A lawyer must not settle a claim or potential claim for such liability with an unrepresented client or former client unless that person is advised in writing of the desirability of seeking, and is given a reasonable opportunity to seek, the advice of independent legal counsel.

Model Rules of Prof'l Conduct R. 1.8(h).

G. **Malpractice Insurance and Risk Prevention**

Insurance companies make malpractice insurance available to lawyers. Lawyers are not required to obtain malpractice insurance.

1) INSURANCE POLICY MAY PROTECT LAWYER FROM LIABILITY

A lawyer may protect himself from financial liability for malpractice by obtaining malpractice insurance. An insurance company issues the policy, which provides coverage in exchange for the payment of premiums.

a) Common Aspects of Insurance Policy

Usually, a legal malpractice insurance policy:

- applies when the insured makes a claim to the insurer (e.g., malpractice lawsuit);
- provides that the insurer will defend the insured;
- covers damages awarded to a plaintiff, such as a former client; and
- may have coverage exclusions (e.g., for pre-existing malpractice).

2)   RISK PREVENTION SEEKS TO DECREASE LIABILITY EXPOSURE

A lawyer should take steps to prevent the risk of legal malpractice actions. Such steps include complying with all applicable law and ethical standards while practicing law. A malpractice insurance provider may inform the insured about risk prevention. For example, the insurer could provide a booklet addressing risk prevention to the insured. The insurer could provide a malpractice insurance application requiring that an applicant describe the applicant's system for identifying prospective clients who present potential problems (e.g., conflicts of interest) that could give rise to legal malpractice actions against the applicant. The applicant could decrease liability exposure by using that system in order to make more informed decisions about whether to represent prospective clients.

COMPETENCE, MALPRACTICE, AND CIVIL LIABILITY

REVIEW QUESTIONS

1. A lawyer not admitted to practice in a jurisdiction is subject to the disciplinary authority of that jurisdiction:
    a. if the lawyer provides or offers to provide legal services in that jurisdiction.
    b. if the lawyer provides consultation to a lawyer licensed to practice in that jurisdiction.
    c. if the lawyer represents himself as a non-licensed lawyer and only offers suggestions.
    d. if the lawyer refers a potential client to a licensed lawyer for a fee.

2. A lawyer may be subject to disciplinary proceedings:
    a. in only the jurisdiction in which the lawyer is licensed.
    b. in more than one jurisdiction for the same conduct.
    c. only if evidence supports a finding of a violation of the Rules beyond a reasonable doubt.
    d. if reported by another lawyer.

3. Civil liability for violating the Rules includes:
    a. automatic forfeiture of a lawyer's license to practice.
    b. causes of action alleging legal malpractice and breach of contract.
    c. statutory fines for repeat violations.
    d. suspension of a lawyer's license to practice law.

4. A legal malpractice claim is a negligence tort claim that is codified in many states. The elements of such a claim are:
    a. duty, breach, causation, damages, and that the lawyer knowingly and intelligently committed the malpractice and failed to self-report the violation.
    b. duty, breach, causation, damages, and that the client would have prevailed in the underlying cause of action that was adversely affected by the lawyer's professional misconduct.
    c. duty, breach, causation, damages.
    d. duty, breach, causation, damages, and that the lawyer knowingly and intelligently committed the malpractice and profited or otherwise benefitted from the actions to the detriment of the client.

5. A lawyer has a duty of professional competence in representation of a client which means that:
    a. the lawyer must possess and maintain competence with regard to those matters of legal representation that the attorney advertises as an area of practice.
    b. the lawyer must possess minimum competency to perform the legal services

> requested.
> c. the lawyer need only maintain continuing legal education relating to legal ethics.
> d. the lawyer possesses and maintains competence in all legal representation, applies reasonable diligence in that representation, and maintains such competence through legal education.

6. Competent representation requires the legal skill, knowledge, thoroughness and preparation needed for the representation. A lawyer should only accept representation if the lawyer can:
    a. apply similar areas of law in which the lawyer is competent to address the client's issues.
    b. project competency to uphold both faith and stability of the legal system while simultaneously engaging other counsel.
    c. competently handle the client's matter or through reasonable preparation can obtain the necessary competence to handle the matter.
    d. file any necessary lawsuit to protect the client's interests, comply with the Statute of Limitations, and refer the client to competent counsel.

7. With respect to a malpractice claim, a lawyer may not:
    a. advise a client of the difficulty of proving a malpractice claim.
    b. reveal possible malpractice concerns with a client which would undermine confidence and trust in the attorney-client relationship.
    c. contract with a client to limit malpractice liability nor attempt to settle a potential malpractice claim without advising the client in writing to obtain independent counsel with respect to the claim and its settlement.
    d. reply to an inquiry from the relevant disciplinary authority concerning a reported incident of malpractice until the complaining client has waived attorney-client confidentiality which prevents an attorney from fully and freely replying.

COMPETENCE, MALPRACTICE, AND CIVIL LIABILITY

ANSWERS TO REVIEW QUESTIONS

Answer 1

The correct answer is choice A. A lawyer not admitted to practice in a jurisdiction is subject to the disciplinary authority of that jurisdiction if the lawyer provides or offers to provide legal services in that jurisdiction.

Answer 2

The correct answer is choice B. A lawyer may be subject to disciplinary proceedings in more than one jurisdiction for the same conduct.

Answer 3

The correct answer is choice B. Civil liability for violating the Rules includes causes of action alleging legal malpractice and breach of contract.

Answer 4

The correct answer is choice B. A legal malpractice claim is a negligence tort claim and is codified in some states. The elements of such a claim are duty, breach, causation, damages, and that the client would have prevailed in the underlying cause of action that was adversely affected by the lawyer's professional misconduct.

Answer 5

The correct answer is choice D. A lawyer has a duty of professional competence in representation of a client which means the lawyer must possess and maintain competence with regard to all legal representation, apply all reasonable diligence to perform the legal services requested, and is obliged to maintain competence via legal education.

Answer 6

The correct answer is choice C. A lawyer should only accept representation if the lawyer can competently handle the client's matter or through reasonable preparation can obtain the necessary competence to handle the matter.

Answer 7

The correct answer is choice C. A lawyer may not contract with a client to limit malpractice liability nor attempt to settle a potential malpractice claim without advising the client in writing to obtain independent counsel with respect to the claim and its settlement.

VI. LITIGATION AND OTHER FORMS OF ADVOCACY

A. Meritorious Claims and Contentions

★   1)   LAWYER CANNOT BRING FRIVOLOUS CLAIM

A lawyer's claims and contentions must have merit. A lawyer can never bring or defend a proceeding, or assert any contention, unless it is grounded in a non-frivolous legal or factual basis. However, a lawyer may make good faith arguments for an extension, modification, or reversal of existing law. Model Rules of Prof'l Conduct R. 3.1.

2)   FEDERAL RULE OF CIVIL PROCEDURE 11

Issues regarding pleadings governed by Federal Rule 11 are usually tested under the subject of Civil Procedure. However, these issues could also arise on the MPRE in relation to meritorious claims and contentions.

a)   Signature Requirement

Every pleading, motion, or other paper of a party represented by an attorney must be *signed* by at least one attorney of record. For a *willful* violation of Federal Rule 11 (failing to sign a pleading or motion), an attorney may be subjected to *disciplinary* action. Incidentally, similar action may be taken if scandalous or indecent matter is inserted.

b)   Representations

When an attorney signs and files a paper with a court, that attorney makes several representations.

(1)   No Improper Purpose

An attorney represents that the contentions set forth in a paper filed with the court are not presented for an improper purpose, such as to harass or to cause unnecessary delay or needless increase in the cost of litigation.

(2)   Legal Grounding

An attorney represents that the legal contentions set forth in a paper filed with the court are warranted by existing law, or by a non-frivolous argument for the extension, modification, or reversal of existing law.

(3)   Evidentiary Support

An attorney represents that the allegations and other factual contentions set forth in a paper filed with the court have evidentiary support or, if specifically so identified, are likely to have evidentiary support after a reasonable opportunity for further investigation or discovery.

(4)   Denials

An attorney represents that the denials of factual contentions set forth in a paper filed with the court are warranted on the evidence or are reasonably based on a lack of information or belief.

c)   Process for Sanctions

A court may sanction an attorney for violating Federal Rule 11. If a court finds that a lawyer violated the Federal Rule 11 representations, then the court may impose an appropriate sanction upon the responsible lawyers, law firms, or parties. The court must give a lawyer notice and a reasonable opportunity to respond.

The court may impose sanctions either by motion or on the court's own initiative.

(1)   By Motion

A party may file a motion for sanctions. A motion for sanctions must describe the specific conduct alleged to violate Federal Rule 11.

(a)   Opportunity to Correct

Before filing a motion for sanctions, a party must provide an opportunity to correct or withdraw the complained-of action. A motion for sanctions must first be served on the parties in the action. It should not be filed with the court at that time. Service of the motion on the parties provides the attorney alleged to have violated the rule with an opportunity to correct the alleged violation. If the complained-of action is not corrected or withdrawn within 21 days after service of the motion on the parties, then the motion may be filed with the court.

(b)   Expenses and Fees Available

If warranted, a court may award, to the party prevailing on the motion, the reasonable expenses and attorney's fees incurred in presenting or opposing the motion.

(2)   On Court's Initiative

A court may enter, on its own initiative, an order describing specific conduct that appears to violate Federal Rule 11. The court may direct the lawyer, law firm, or party to withdraw or correct the violative contentions or show cause why it has not violated Federal Rule 11.

(d)   Nature of Sanctions

A sanction imposed for violation of Federal Rule 11 is limited to that which is sufficient to deter repetition of the conduct or comparable conduct by others. The sanction may include directives of a nonmonetary nature and an order to pay a penalty to court. A court may also order an attorney violating Federal Rule 11 to pay, to the moving party, reasonable attorney's fees and expenses incurred as a direct result of the violation.

B.   Expediting Litigation

A lawyer must make reasonable efforts to expedite litigation consistent with the interests of a client. Model Rules of Prof'l Conduct R. 3.2. This obligation goes hand-in-hand with the lawyer's duty of diligence.

★★   ## C.   Candor to the Tribunal

An attorney must act with openness and honesty to a tribunal. A "tribunal" is a court, an arbitrator in a binding arbitration proceeding, a legislative body, an administrative agency, or any other body acting in an adjudicative capacity. Model Rules of Prof'l Conduct R. 1.0.

1)   FALSE REPRESENTATIONS ARE PROHIBITED

A lawyer cannot knowingly make false statements, fail to disclose binding legal authority, or provide false evidence to a tribunal.

a)   False Statements

A lawyer cannot make a false statement of material fact or law to a tribunal, or fail to correct a false statement of material fact or law the lawyer previously made to the tribunal.

b)   Binding Legal Authority

A lawyer cannot fail to disclose to the tribunal legal authority in the controlling jurisdiction known to the lawyer to be *directly adverse* to the position of the client and not disclosed by opposing counsel.

c)   False Evidence

A lawyer cannot knowingly offer false evidence. If a lawyer, the lawyer's client, or a witness called by the lawyer has offered material evidence and the lawyer comes to know of its falsity, the lawyer must take reasonable remedial measures, including, if necessary, disclosure to the tribunal. The lawyer may refuse to offer evidence, other than the testimony of a defendant in a criminal matter, that the lawyer reasonably believes is false. Model Rules of Prof'l Conduct R. 3.3(a).

2)   LAWYER'S SUBSEQUENT REMEDIAL MEASURES

A lawyer who represents a client in an adjudicative proceeding and who knows that the client intends to engage in, is engaging in, or has engaged in criminal or fraudulent conduct related to the proceeding, must take reasonable remedial measures, including, if necessary, disclosure to the tribunal. Model Rules of Prof'l Conduct R. 3.3(b).

a) Duration of Duties

The duty to take reasonable remedial measures continues until the proceeding's conclusion and applies even if compliance requires disclosure of information otherwise protected by the Rule of Confidentiality. Model Rules of Prof'l Conduct R. 3.3(c).

3) DISCLOSURE OF MATERIAL FACTS IN *EX-PARTE* PROCEEDINGS

In an *ex-parte* proceeding, a lawyer must disclose all known material facts to the tribunal that will enable the tribunal to make an informed decision. Model Rules of Prof'l Conduct R. 3.3(d).

D. Fairness to Opposing Party and Counsel

The concepts of civility, courtesy, and decorum are not just pleasant notions about polite behavior among professionals. Those concepts have practical application in maintaining the appropriate level of professional propriety in the conduct of legal proceedings.

A lawyer must be fair to an opposing party and counsel. The fairness required under the ethical rules impacts the lawyer's conduct in all phases of litigation.

1) EVIDENCE

a) Access to Evidence

A lawyer cannot obstruct a party's access to evidence or material having potential evidentiary value.

b) Falsification of Evidence

A lawyer cannot falsify evidence, counsel or assist a witness to testify falsely, or offer an inducement to a witness that is prohibited by law.

c) Discovery Requests

A lawyer cannot make a frivolous discovery request or fail to make a reasonably diligent effort to comply with a legally proper discovery request by an opposing party.

d) Request to Not Disclose Relevant Information

A lawyer cannot request that a person other than a client refrain from voluntarily giving relevant information to another party unless the person is a relative or an agent of a client, and the lawyer reasonably believes that the person's interests will not be adversely affected by refraining from giving such information.

2) TRIAL

In trial, a lawyer cannot allude to any matter that the lawyer does not reasonably believe is relevant or that will not be supported by admissible evidence. A lawyer cannot assert personal knowledge of facts in issue except when testifying as a witness or state a personal opinion as to the justness of a cause, the credibility of a witness, the culpability of a civil litigant, or the guilt or innocence of an accused. However, some courts permit an attorney to assert that a witness lied if that assertion is supported by the facts.

3) DISOBEY RULES OF TRIBUNAL

A lawyer cannot knowingly disobey an obligation under the rules of a tribunal except for an open refusal based on an assertion that no valid obligation exists.

4) THREATS

a) Criminal Charges

A lawyer cannot present (or threaten to present) criminal charges in order to obtain an advantage in a civil matter.

b) Disciplinary Charges

A lawyer cannot present (or threaten to present) disciplinary charges under the ethical rules in order to obtain an advantage in a civil matter.

Model Rules of Prof'l Conduct R. 3.4.

As allowed by law, a lawyer may pay for a witness's reasonable expenses, but the lawyer may not pay the witness for the witness's testimony. An expert witness, however, may be paid for the expert's time in testifying, but the fee paid to the expert must be a non-contingent fee. *Id.*, cmt. [3].

E. Impartiality and Decorum of the Tribunal

★★ ### 1) IMPROPER CONTACT WITH COURT AND JURORS

A lawyer must avoid improper contact with court officials and jurors. A lawyer cannot communicate or attempt to influence a judge, juror, prospective juror, or other judicial official. Even after a trial is concluded, a lawyer cannot communicate with a juror if the juror has demonstrated a desire not to communicate. Of course, a lawyer is always prohibited from engaging in conduct intended to disrupt a tribunal.

Model Rules of Prof'l Conduct R. 3.5.

 ### F. Trial Publicity

1) NO PREJUDICIAL EXTRAJUDICIAL STATEMENTS

A lawyer who is participating, or has participated, in the investigation or litigation of a matter must not make an extrajudicial (out of court) statement that the lawyer knows or reasonably should know will be disseminated by means of public communication and will have a substantial likelihood of materially prejudicing an adjudicative proceeding in the matter. Model Rules of Prof'l Conduct R. 3.6(a).

a) Exception for Responsive Statement

A lawyer may make a statement that a reasonable lawyer would believe is required to protect a client from the substantial undue prejudicial effect of recent publicity not initiated by the lawyer or the lawyer's client. Such a statement must be limited to the information necessary to mitigate the recent adverse publicity. Model Rules of Prof'l Conduct R. 3.6(c).

★★ G. Lawyer as Witness

Generally, a lawyer should not represent a client in a matter in which the lawyer might need to testify. Specifically, a lawyer cannot act as advocate at a trial in which the lawyer is likely to be a necessary witness unless:

- the testimony relates to an uncontested issue;
- the testimony relates to the nature and value of legal services provided; or
- the lawyer's disqualification would be a substantial hardship to the client.

Model Rules of Prof'l Conduct R. 3.7(a).

LITIGATION AND OTHER FORMS OF ADVOCACY

REVIEW QUESTIONS

1. A lawyer should not represent a client if the lawyer is likely to be a necessary witness except when:
    a. the lawyer's testimony relates to an uncontested issue, the lawyer's testimony relates to value of services provided, or the lawyer's disqualification would work a substantial hardship on the client.
    b. the client expressly waives any claim against the lawyer as a result of the testimony proving harmful to the client.
    c. the lawyer is confident that the lawyer's testimony will not reveal any attorney-client privileged information.
    d. a neutral magistrate hears the testimony in camera and determines the lawyer as a witness is necessary to the client.

2. A lawyer should behave with:
    a. the proper manners demonstrated by other lawyers, judges and elected officials.
    b. due respect and in accordance with the local rules and customs of the court before which the lawyer is practicing.
    c. civility, courtesy, and decorum which are legal standards that must be respected.
    d. the reasonable manners expected of anyone in a position of trust and authority.

3. A lawyer must act in fairness to opposing parties and counsel, meaning a lawyer, among other things:
    a. cannot unlawfully obstruct access to evidence, or destroy or alter anything of evidentiary value, make a frivolous discovery request or obstruct a valid discovery request, nor assist in false testimony or make any unlawful inducement to a witness.
    b. cannot make objections throughout a trial that lengthen the trial and delay a decision.
    c. cannot file lengthy and detailed motions that make opposing counsel's work more difficult than a reasonably competent attorney of similar education and experience might otherwise do.
    d. cannot act in a zealous manner that the lawyer knows will enflame the passions of the opposing party.

4. The rule requiring a lawyer to act with impartiality and make only meritorious claims and contentions allows the lawyer to:
    a. bring a proceeding in which there are serious questions about the laws or facts underlying the case.
    b. make good faith arguments for reversals, modification, or extensions of existing law.

    c. challenge a prior court ruling against a client where the judge held the client in contempt.

    d. file claims based solely on the word of the client if the client has financial means to support a suit.

5. A lawyer makes the following representations when making a filing:

    a. the filing conforms to the proper document size and all court rules relating to its formatting.

    b. the lawyer has verified the veracity of the client's statements which are the basis of the filing.

    c. there is no improper purpose, the filing rests on a legal grounding, and there is evidentiary support for the filing.

    d. no reasonable denials of factual contentions are warranted on the evidence.

6. Improper filings may be the subject of:

    a. sanctions requested by opposing counsel or imposed by the court sufficient to deter repetition of the offensive conduct or comparable conduct by others.

    b. sanctions requiring payment of fines and jail time.

    c. review and rejection by the court which can force counsel to refile properly.

    d. lost profits due to the fact that an attorney may have to redo work and absorb the added expense.

7. A lawyer may not compensate a witness for the witness's time, with the exception of:

    a. witnesses who travel more than 100 miles to testify.

    b. witnesses who are reasonably fearful for their safety as a result of their testimony and, therefore, require law enforcement protection.

    c. expert witnesses, who can be paid a non-contingent fee.

    d. expert witnesses who waive their fee but accept a reasonably negotiated percentage of any award secured by the party for whom they are testifying.

8. A lawyer's duty of candor requires that the lawyer:

    a. exhibit a calm demeanor and respectful tone before the court.

    b. must be blunt and direct when speaking to the court.

    c. disclose controlling cases or law directly opposed to a client's interest, even if opposing counsel fails to disclose them.

    d. withhold controlling cases or law detrimental to a client's interest if opposing counsel fails to disclose them.

9. A lawyer must take subsequent remedial measures if the lawyer knows or reasonably believes that the client will take criminal or fraudulent actions related to the proceedings. Such subsequent remedial measures include:

    a. disclosure of such conduct to the court and even disclosure of confidential information.

    b. withdrawing from representation of the client.

    c. notifying adverse parties of the client's actions so that the adverse parties can protect themselves.

d. documenting the client's words and actions as proof and the lawyer's own words and actions attempting to prevent the client from causing further harm.

LITIGATION AND OTHER FORMS OF ADVOCACY

ANSWERS TO REVIEW QUESTIONS

Answer 1

The correct answer is choice A. A lawyer should not represent a client if the lawyer is likely to be a necessary witness except if the lawyer's testimony relates to an uncontested issue, the lawyer's testimony relates to value of services provided, or the lawyer's disqualification would work a substantial hardship on the client.

Answer 2

The correct answer is choice C. A lawyer should behave with civility, courtesy, and decorum which are legal standards that must be respected.

Answer 3

The correct answer is choice A. A lawyer must act in fairness to opposing parties and counsel, meaning a lawyer, among other things, cannot unlawfully obstruct access to evidence, or destroy or alter anything of evidentiary value, make a frivolous discovery request or obstruct a valid discovery request, nor assist in false testimony or make any unlawful inducement to a witness.

Answer 4

The correct answer is choice B. The rule requiring a lawyer to act with impartiality and make only meritorious claims and contentions allows the lawyer to make good faith arguments for reversals, modification, or extensions of existing law.

Answer 5

The correct answer is choice C. When making a filing, a lawyer represents that there is no improper purpose, the filing rests on a legal grounding, and there is evidentiary support for the filing.

Answer 6

The correct answer is choice A. Improper filings may be the subject of sanctions requested by opposing counsel or imposed by the court sufficient to deter repetition of the offensive conduct or comparable conduct by others.

Answer 7

The correct answer is choice C. A lawyer many not compensate a witness for more than the witness's reasonable expenses. However, expert witnesses can be paid a non-contingent fee for the expert's time.

Answer 8

The correct answer is choice C. A lawyer's duty of candor requires that the lawyer disclose controlling cases or law directly opposed to a client's interest, even if opposing counsel fails to disclose them.

Answer 9

The correct answer is choice A. A lawyer must take subsequent remedial measures if the lawyer knows or reasonably believes that the client will take criminal or fraudulent actions related to the proceedings. Such subsequent remedial measures include disclosure of such conduct to the court and even disclosure of confidential information.

VII. COMMUNICATIONS WITH PERSONS OTHER THAN CLIENTS

★

A. Truthfulness in Statements to Others

1) NO FALSE STATEMENTS OF FACT

A lawyer must never knowingly make a false statement of material fact or law to a third person. A misrepresentation may qualify as a false statement of material fact. A lawyer makes a prohibited misrepresentation if the lawyer affirms another person's statement that the lawyer knows is false, even if the lawyer does not specifically say something false.

For example, suppose a client and lawyer are having lunch together when they are approached by an opponent's attorney. If the client tells the attorney a material fact that the attorney knows is false, and the attorney nods in affirmation, the act of nodding could be interpreted as a false statement of fact.

2) NO FAILURE TO DISCLOSE MATERIAL FACT ASSISTING CRIME

A lawyer must never fail to disclose a material fact when disclosure is necessary to avoid assisting a criminal or fraudulent act by a client, unless disclosure is prohibited by the Rule of Confidentiality. Model Rules of Prof'l Conduct R. 4.1. The rule only applies when the disclosure is required to prevent a fraudulent or criminal act by the client. Therefore, a lawyer has no general affirmative duty to inform an opposing party of relevant facts.

3) DISTINGUISHING STATEMENTS MADE DURING NEGOTIATIONS

Some statements made during negotiations are not treated as statements of fact. For example, estimates of price or value, and a party's intentions as to an acceptable settlement offer of a claim are ordinarily in this category. For example, a lawyer can tell opposing counsel that a client wouldn't accept a settlement offer below $1,000,000, even if the lawyer knows this is not truth.

★

B. Communications with Represented Persons

In representing a client, a lawyer must not communicate about the subject of the representation with a person the lawyer knows to be represented by another lawyer in the matter, unless the lawyer has the other lawyer's consent or is authorized to do so by law or a court order. Model Rules of Prof'l Conduct R. 4.2.

★★

C. Communications with Unrepresented Persons

In dealing on behalf of a client with a person who is not represented by counsel, a lawyer must not state or imply that the lawyer is disinterested. When the lawyer knows or reasonably should know that the unrepresented person misunderstands the lawyer's role in the matter, the lawyer must make reasonable efforts to correct the misunderstanding. The lawyer must not give legal advice to an unrepresented person, other than the advice to secure counsel if the lawyer knows, or reasonably should know, that the interests of such a person are, or have a reasonable possibility of becoming, in conflict with the interests of the client. Model Rules of Prof'l Conduct R. 4.3.

D.   Respect for Rights of Third Persons

1)   HARASSING OTHERS

In representing a client, a lawyer must not use means that have no substantial purpose other than to embarrass, delay, or burden a third person, or use methods of obtaining evidence that violate the legal rights of such a person. Model Rules of Prof'l Conduct R. 4.4(a).

2)   INADVERTENT DISCLOSURE OF INFORMATION

Special problems are presented when a document is inadvertently sent by a non-client to a lawyer. The document can be sent in various ways including mail, fax, email, or other electronic modes. Model Rules of Prof'l Conduct R. 4.4 cmt. [2].
Specifically, a lawyer who receives a document related to the representation of the lawyer's client and knows or reasonably should know that the document was inadvertently sent must promptly notify the sender. Model Rules of Prof'l Conduct R. 4.4(b).

If the inadvertently sent document contains confidential or privileged information about an opposing party (the sender or the sender's client), the receiving lawyer should "promptly notify the sender in order to permit that person to take protective measures." Model Rules of Prof'l Conduct R. 4.4 cmt. [2].

If the document includes confidential or privileged information, the sender may request a protective order from the relevant court. If the court declines to issue the protective order, the receiving party could possibly use the information against the sender and/or the sender's client. The law is unsettled as to whether the privilege is lost after accidental disclosure and whether the court should protect the sender from the consequences of such disclosure. A consideration that could affect the court's decision on this issue is whether the sender took reasonable precautions to prevent the inadvertent disclosure.

COMMUNICATIONS WITH PERSONS OTHER THAN CLIENTS

REVIEW QUESTIONS

1. Can a lawyer communicate about a legal matter with a person involved in the matter who is known to be represented by an attorney?
   a. Never.
   b. No, unless authorized by the law or a court order.
   c. Yes, if the attorney has the informed consent of the represented party.
   d. Yes, if the attorney has the other lawyer's consent or is authorized by law or court order.

2. A lawyer who obtains confidential information through an inadvertent disclosure by a third party must:
   a. prudently use the information to the client's benefit if not doing so would prejudice or harm the client's case and possibly result in malpractice.
   b. acknowledge receipt of the information in writing to the third party.
   c. notify the third party sender if the lawyer knows or should know the information was inadvertently sent.
   d. seek a court's protective order to allow fair use of the inadvertent disclosure.

COMMUNICATIONS WITH PERSONS OTHER THAN CLIENTS

ANSWERS TO REVIEW QUESTIONS

Answer 1

The correct answer is choice D. In representing a client, a lawyer must not communicate about the subject of the representation with a person the lawyer knows to be represented by another lawyer in the matter, unless the lawyer has the other lawyer's consent or is authorized to do so by law or a court order.

Answer 2

The correct answer is choice C. A lawyer who obtains confidential information through an inadvertent disclosure by a third party must notify the third party sender if the lawyer knows or should know the information was inadvertently sent.

VIII.   DIFFERENT ROLES OF THE LAWYER

A lawyer performs various functions in several different capacities. For example, as an advocate, a lawyer zealously represents a client's interest. As an advisor, a lawyer provides a client with an informed understanding of legal rights and responsibilities and explains practical implications.

A.   Lawyer as Advisor

In representing a client, a lawyer must exercise independent professional judgment and provide candid advice. In providing advice, a lawyer may refer not only to law but to other considerations such as moral, economic, social, and political factors that may be relevant to the client's situation. Model Rules of Prof'l Conduct R. 2.1.

B.   Lawyer as Evaluator

As an evaluator, a lawyer examines a client's legal affairs and reports about them to the client.

1)   EVALUATION FOR USE BY THIRD PERSONS

A lawyer may provide an evaluation of a matter affecting a client for the use of someone other than the client if the lawyer reasonably believes that making the evaluation is compatible with other aspects of the lawyer's relationship with the client. Model Rules of Prof'l Conduct R. 2.3(a).

When the lawyer knows, or reasonably should know, that the evaluation is likely to affect the client's interests materially and adversely, the lawyer must not provide the evaluation unless the client gives informed consent. Model Rules of Prof'l Conduct R. 2.3(b).

Information relating to the evaluation is otherwise protected by the Rule of Confidentiality. Model Rules of Prof'l Conduct R. 2.3(c).

C.   Lawyer as Negotiator

As negotiator, a lawyer seeks a result advantageous to the client. However, the lawyer must deal honestly with others.

D.   Lawyer as Arbitrator, Mediator, or Other Third-Party Neutral

In addition to acting as a representative, a lawyer may serve as a third-party neutral, a nonrepresentational role helping the parties to resolve a dispute or other matter. A lawyer serves as a third-party neutral when the lawyer assists two or more people who are not clients of the lawyer to reach a resolution of a dispute or other matter that has arisen between them. Service as a third-party neutral may include service as an arbitrator, a mediator, or in such other capacity as will enable the lawyer to assist the parties to resolve the matter. Model Rules of Prof'l Conduct R. 2.4(a).

A lawyer serving as a third-party neutral must inform unrepresented parties that the lawyer is not representing them. When the lawyer knows or reasonably should know that a party does not understand the lawyer's role in the matter, the lawyer must explain the difference between the lawyer's role as a third-party neutral and a lawyer's role as one who represents a client. Model Rules of Prof'l Conduct R. 2.4(b).

★   **E.   Prosecutors and Other Governmental Lawyers**

1)   SPECIAL RESPONSIBILITIES OF PROSECUTORS DURING CASE

A prosecutor possesses special responsibilities regarding the prosecution of a criminal action. The prosecutor in a criminal case must:

- refrain from prosecuting a charge that the prosecutor knows is not supported by probable cause;
- make reasonable efforts to assure that the accused has been advised of the right to, and the procedure for obtaining, counsel, and has been given reasonable opportunity to obtain counsel;
- not seek to obtain from an unrepresented accused a waiver of important pretrial rights, such as the right to a preliminary hearing;
- make timely disclosure to the defense of all evidence or information known to the prosecutor that tends to negate the guilt of the accused or mitigates the offense, and, in connection with sentencing, disclose to the defense and to the tribunal all unprivileged mitigating information known to the prosecutor, except when the prosecutor is relieved of this responsibility by a protective order of the tribunal;
- not subpoena a lawyer in a grand jury or other criminal proceeding to present evidence about a past or present client unless the prosecutor reasonably believes:

     (1)   the information sought is not protected from disclosure by any applicable privilege;

     (2)   the evidence sought is essential to the successful completion of an ongoing investigation or prosecution; and

     (3)   there is no other feasible alternative to obtain the information.

Model Rules of Prof'l Conduct R. 3.8(a)-(e).

2)   DUTY OF PROSECUTOR TO DISCLOSE INFORMATION CONCERNING CONVICTION

a)   New Credible and Material Evidence

When a prosecutor knows of new credible and material evidence creating a reasonable likelihood that a convicted defendant did not commit the offense, the prosecutor must promptly disclose the evidence to an appropriate court or authority. If the conviction was obtained in the prosecutor's jurisdiction, then the prosecutor must promptly disclose the evidence to the defendant unless a court authorizes delay. Additionally, the prosecutor must undertake further investigation, or make reasonable efforts to cause an investigation, to determine whether the defendant was convicted of an offense that the defendant did not commit.

b) Clear and Convincing Evidence

When a prosecutor knows of clear and convincing evidence establishing that a defendant in the prosecutor's jurisdiction was convicted of an offense that the defendant did not commit, the prosecutor must seek to remedy the conviction.

3) DUTY OF PROSECUTOR TO REFRAIN FROM MAKING EXTRAJUDICIAL COMMENTS

Except for statements that serve a legitimate law enforcement purpose, a prosecutor must refrain from making extrajudicial comments that have a substantial likelihood of heightening public condemnation of the accused. A prosecutor must also exercise reasonable care to prevent investigators, law enforcement personnel, employees, or other persons assisting or associated with the prosecutor in a criminal case from making an extrajudicial statement that the prosecutor would be prohibited from making.

★★ ## F. Lawyer Appearing in Non-Adjudicative Proceeding

A lawyer representing a client before a legislative body or administrative agency in a non-adjudicative proceeding must: 1) disclose that the appearance is in a representative capacity; and 2) conform to the Rules regarding Candor toward the Tribunal, Fairness to Opposing Party and Counsel, and Impartiality and Decorum of the Tribunal. Model Rules of Prof'l Conduct R. 3.9.

★★ ## G. Lawyer Representing an Entity or Other Organization

An organization is an entity such as a business, company, corporation, or other entity. A lawyer can represent an individual or an organization. Special rules apply to representing an organization as a client.

1) GENERAL DUTY TO ORGANIZATION

When a lawyer represents an organization, the lawyer owes a fiduciary duty to the *organization* itself. Such a duty is paramount to any duty to the individual officers, directors, or employees of the organization. Accordingly, a lawyer employed or retained by an organization represents the organization acting through its duly authorized constituents. Model Rules of Prof'l Conduct R. 1.13(a).

2) VIOLATIONS OF LEGAL OBLIGATIONS OR LAWS

If a lawyer for an organization knows that an officer, employee or other person associated with the organization is engaged in action, intends to act, or refuses to act in a matter related to the representation that is a violation of a legal obligation to the organization, or a violation of law that reasonably might be imputed to the organization, and that is likely to result in substantial injury to the organization, the lawyer must proceed as is reasonably necessary in the best interest of the organization. Model Rules of Prof'l Conduct R. 1.13(b).

Unless the lawyer reasonably believes that it is not necessary in the best interest of the organization to do so, the lawyer *must* refer the matter to higher authority in the organization, including, if warranted by the circumstances, to the highest authority that can act on behalf of the organization (such as the board of directors) as determined by applicable law. *Id.*

3) ADVERSE ORGANIZATION AND CONSTITUENTS

In dealing with an organization's directors, officers, employees, members, shareholders or other constituents, a lawyer must explain the identity of the client when the lawyer knows or reasonably should know that the organization's interests are adverse to those of the constituents with whom the lawyer is dealing. Model Rules of Prof'l Conduct R. 1.13(f).

4) DUAL REPRESENTATION

A lawyer representing an organization may also represent any of its directors, officers, employees, members, shareholders or other constituents, subject to the provisions of the Rule regarding conflicts of interest involving current clients. If the organization's consent to the dual representation is required by that Rule, the consent must be given by an appropriate official of the organization other than the individual who is to be represented, or by the shareholders. Model Rules of Prof'l Conduct R. 1.13(g).

DIFFERENT ROLES OF THE LAWYER

REVIEW QUESTIONS

1. A lawyer may serve in the role of negotiator, mediator, arbitrator, or some other form of third-party neutral while assisting two or more people who are not clients to reach a resolution of a dispute. In such a capacity, the lawyer must:
    a. advise all parties of their constitutional rights under the proceedings.
    b. inform unrepresented parties that the lawyer is not representing them and explain the role of a third-party neutral.
    c. discuss the possible admissions and denials the parties may make and the effect each may have on the proceeding and the party.
    d. reach a successful conclusion that avoids a formal trial.

2. A prosecutor must:
    a. refrain from prosecuting a charge that's not supported by reasonable suspicion.
    b. make timely disclosure to the defense of all evidence that mitigates the offense or tends to negate the guilt of the accused.
    c. prosecute all crimes and misdemeanors supported by some credible evidence with the knowledge that the discovery process is likely to reveal further useful information.
    d. make reasonable efforts to meet with the accused and the accused's counsel prior to trial in order to negotiate a plea agreement and reduce unnecessary public expenditures on legal fees and costs.

3. When representing an organization, a lawyer owes a fiduciary duty to:
    a. the Board of Directors, which is ultimately responsible for all aspects of the organization.
    b. the CEO responsible for all day-to-day operations of the organization.
    c. the organization itself and not any officer or director.
    d. all persons employed by the organization who will be affected by the lawyer's representation.

4. If a lawyer representing an organization has knowledge that an employee of the organization intends to act, or will act, in a manner that is detrimental to the organization, the lawyer must:
    a. advise the person considering acting in a manner detrimental to the organization that, as a lawyer for the organization, the lawyer will not allow the person to take such action.
    b. proceed as is reasonably necessary in the best interest of the organization.
    c. notify the individual that the lawyer will take legal action against the individual to prevent any possible action that is detrimental to the organization.
    d. inform the person's superior that the person's employment should be terminated

prior to the person taking action detrimental to the organization.

5.   A lawyer may agree to "dual representation" (representing both an organization and a representative of the organization) if:
   a.   the lawyer representing the organization has another lawyer in the same firm represent the representative of the organization.
   b.   there are no conflicts of interests and, if consent is required under a conflict of interest rule, it is given by an appropriate representative of the organization or the shareholders.
   c.   the dual representation is presented to a neutral magistrate for review and the court determines there is no conflict.
   d.   the lawyer is paid by both the organization and the representative of the organization, but from separate sources of funding to avoid commingling of client funds.

DIFFERENT ROLES OF THE LAWYER

ANSWERS TO REVIEW QUESTIONS

Answer 1

The correct answer is choice B. In the role of negotiator, mediator, arbitrator, or some other form of third-party neutral while assisting two or more people who are not clients to reach a resolution of a dispute, a lawyer must inform unrepresented parties that the lawyer is not representing them and explain the role of a third-party neutral.

Answer 2

The correct answer is choice B. Prosecutors must make timely disclosure to the defense of all evidence that mitigates the offense or tends to negate the guilt of the accused.

Answer 3
The correct answer is choice C. When representing the organization, a lawyer owes a paramount fiduciary duty to the organization itself and not to any particular person within the organization.

Answer 4
The correct answer is choice B. A lawyer representing an organization must proceed as is reasonably necessary in the best interest of the organization if the lawyer has knowledge that any employee of an organization intends to act or will act in a manner that is detrimental to the organization.

Answer 5
The correct answer is choice B. If there are no conflicts of interest and, if required, consent is given by an appropriate representative of the organization or the shareholders, a lawyer may undertake dual representation of both an organization and a representative of the organization.

IX. SAFEKEEPING FUNDS AND OTHER PROPERTY

A. Establishing and Maintaining Client Trust Accounts

1) CLIENT TRUST ACCOUNTS

When a lawyer holds property of clients or third persons in connection with legal representation, the lawyer must keep that property *separate* from the lawyer's own property. Model Rules of Prof'l Conduct R. 1.15(a). For exam purposes, the implicated property is usually money in a bank account. For example, unearned retainers must be placed in a separate client trust account. A lawyer must deposit into this client trust account legal fees and expenses that have been paid in advance, to be withdrawn by the lawyer only as fees are earned or expenses incurred. Model Rules of Prof'l Conduct R. 1.15(c). Separate trust accounts may be warranted when administering estates or acting in another similar fiduciary capacity.

a) Account Located in State of Office

Funds must be kept in a separate client trust account in the state where the lawyer's office is located, or elsewhere with the consent of the client or third person.

b) Complete Records Must be Kept for Five Years

A lawyer must keep complete records of client trust account funds and other property. The records must be preserved for five years after termination of the legal representation.

c) Limited Exception for Paying Bank Service Charges

A lawyer can deposit the lawyer's own funds in a client trust account for the sole purpose of paying bank service charges on that account, but only in an amount necessary for that purpose. Model Rules of Prof'l Conduct R. 1.15(b). Under other circumstances, though, mixing the lawyer's own funds with client funds in a client trust account is not permitted and can result in prohibited commingling of those funds. Model Rules of Prof'l Conduct R. 1.15 cmt. [2].

B. Safekeeping Funds and Other Property of Clients

1) SEPARATION OF PROPERTY

A lawyer should hold property of others with the care required of a professional fiduciary. As a general matter, securities should be kept in a safe deposit box, except when some other form of safekeeping is warranted by special circumstances.

C. Safekeeping Funds and Other Property of Third Persons

Attorneys often receive money from third parties from which the lawyer's fee will ultimately be paid. For example, a lawyer may receive a settlement check, from which the lawyer's fee will be paid. Upon receiving funds or other property in which a client or third person has an interest, a lawyer must promptly notify the client or third person. Model Rules of Prof'l Conduct R. 1.15(d).

Unless the Rules, the law, or an agreement provides otherwise, a lawyer must promptly deliver to the client or third person any funds or property the client or third person is entitled to receive and, upon request by the client or third person, must promptly provide a full accounting regarding such property. *Id.*

★★ **D.** **Disputed Claims**

1) TYPES OF DISPUTES

The following types of disputes can arise regarding claims upon property contained in client trust funds:

- The lawyer and the client might disagree about the amount of funds in the account that the lawyer can keep as earnings for services provided to the client.

- The lawyer might disagree with the client's creditor regarding the amount of funds to which the creditor claims it is entitled pursuant to the client's alleged obligation.

- The client's creditor might disagree with the client regarding their respective claims to the funds in the account.

2) CONTROL OF FUNDS

a) Funds Must Be Separate

When in the course of representation a lawyer is in possession of property in which two or more people claim interests, the property must be kept separate by the lawyer until the dispute is resolved. Model Rules of Prof'l Conduct R. 1.15(e). One of the people claiming an interest in the property can be the lawyer. *Id.*

b) Undisputed Funds Must Be Promptly Returned

In the event of a disputed claim, the lawyer must promptly distribute the remaining, undisputed portion of the property. *Id.*

c) Lawyer can Withhold Funds for Fees if Risk Exists

If there is risk that the client may divert funds without paying the fee, the lawyer is not required to remit the portion from which the fee is to be paid. However, a lawyer may not hold funds to coerce a client into accepting the lawyer's contention.

d) Dispute Between Client and Third Party

A lawyer may be obligated to protect a third-party's lawful claims upon a client's funds or property, which the lawyer possesses, from a client's wrongful interference. *Id.*, cmt. [4]. In that event, if the third-party's claim is not frivolous, the lawyer may not release the funds or property to the client until resolution of the competing claims occurs. *Id.* The lawyer may not assume to decide a dispute between the third party and the client. *Id.* However, the lawyer can file an action to have a court resolve their dispute when substantial grounds exist for the dispute. *Id.* For example, suppose a client is awarded damages in a civil action that have been transferred to the lawyer for distribution to the client. If a third-party creditor possesses a lien on those funds, the lawyer must protect the funds. *Id.*

SAFEKEEPING FUNDS AND OTHER PROPERTY

REVIEW QUESTIONS

1. A lawyer must hold client funds as a fiduciary and keep them separate from the lawyer's own funds. However,
    a. retainers are up-front payments to the lawyer who may access them as needed for business purposes.
    b. a lawyer must provide a full accounting of the client's funds within two business days of such a demand by the client.
    c. a lawyer need not set aside funds that are in dispute with a client as the lawyer can always return the funds when the dispute is settled.
    d. a lawyer can deposit the lawyer's own funds in a client trust account for the sole purpose of paying bank service charges on that account.

SAFEKEEPING FUNDS AND OTHER PROPERTY

ANSWERS TO REVIEW QUESTIONS

Answer 1

The correct answer is choice D. A lawyer must hold client funds as a fiduciary and keep them separate from the lawyer's own funds. However, a lawyer can deposit the lawyer's own funds in a client trust account for the sole purpose of paying bank service charges on that account.

X. COMMUNICATION ABOUT LEGAL SERVICES

★★★★

A. Advertising and Other Public Communications About Legal Services

Historically, ethical rules prohibited lawyers from advertising their services. Today, lawyers are permitted to conduct limited advertising.

★★★
1) COMMUNICATIONS CONCERNING A LAWYER'S SERVICES

a) Must Be Truthful

A lawyer cannot make a false or misleading communication about the lawyer or the lawyer's services. Model Rules of Prof'l Conduct R. 7.1. A communication is false or misleading if it contains a material misrepresentation of fact or law, or omits a fact necessary to make the statement considered as a whole not materially misleading. *Id.*

b) Unjustified Expectations

A lawyer may not include statements of fact or opinion that would create an unjustified expectation. An example of such a statement is that "opposing counsel shiver when they hear that I represent the plaintiff."

c) Unfair Comparisons

An advertisement may not include unfair comparisons to other lawyers.

★★★
2) ADVERTISING

Subject to the requirement of truthful (and not false or misleading) statements and the limitations upon directly contacting prospective clients, a lawyer may advertise services through written, recorded, or electronic communication, including public media. Model Rules of Prof'l Conduct R. 7.2(a).

a) Contents of Advertisements

Most types of advertisements must contain the name and office address of the lawyer or law firm responsible for the contents of the advertisement. Model Rules of Prof'l Conduct R. 7.2(c). Additionally, an advertisement may not mention a client *unless* the client is regularly represented by that lawyer or firm and the client consents in advance. *Id.*, cmt. [2].

b) Keeping Copies of Advertisements

In many jurisdictions, a lawyer must keep copies of written or electronic advertisements for two years. The copies must be produced on demand from the state regulatory authorities.

c) Place of Advertisements

In many jurisdictions, a court may consider the location of the advertisement in determining its permissibility. For example, an advertisement located in a hospital will generally not be permitted because of the potentially vulnerable nature of the patients.

★★ ### 3) FIRM NAMES AND LETTERHEAD

a) Not False or Misleading

A lawyer must not use a firm name, letterhead, or other professional designation that is false or misleading. Model Rules of Prof'l Conduct R. 7.5(a). A trade name may be used by a lawyer in private practice if it does not imply a connection with a government agency or with a public or charitable legal services organization and is not otherwise false or misleading. *Id.*

b) Partner Serving in Public Office

The name of a lawyer holding a public office cannot be used in the name of a law firm, or in communications on its behalf, during any substantial period in which the lawyer is not actively and regularly practicing with the firm. Model Rules of Prof'l Conduct R. 7.5(c).

c) Representation as Partnership

Lawyers may state or imply that they practice in a partnership or other organization only when that is the fact. Model Rules of Prof'l Conduct R. 7.5(d).

d) Jurisdiction Admissions

A law firm with offices in more than one jurisdiction may use the same name or other professional designation in each jurisdiction, but identification of the lawyers in an office of the firm must indicate the jurisdictional limitations on those not licensed to practice in the jurisdiction where the office is located. Model Rules of Prof'l Conduct R. 7.5(b).

★ ## B. Solicitation – Direct Contact with Prospective Clients

1) REAL-TIME SOLICITATION PROHIBITED

Unlike advertising, as a general rule, real time solicitation is prohibited. A lawyer may not by in-person, live telephone, or real-time electronic contact solicit professional employment when a significant motive for doing so is the lawyer's pecuniary gain. Model Rules of Prof'l Conduct R. 7.3(a).

a) Exception to Prohibition

The prohibition is not applicable if the person solicited is:1) a lawyer; or 2) has a family, close personal, or prior professional relationship with the lawyer. *Id.*

2)   OTHER SOLICITATION PERMISSIBLE

Solicitation that is not real-time (i.e., not in person), on the telephone, or real-time electronic contact, is permissible. So solicitation by direct mail or electronic mail or by other electronic means that do not involve real time contact may be permissible, if not otherwise prohibited. Model Rules of Prof'l Conduct R. 7.3(b) cmt. [3].

a)   Exception to Allowable Solicitations

A lawyer may not solicit professional employment by *written,* recorded, or electronic communication or by in-person, telephone, or real-time electronic contact if: 1) the target of the solicitation has made known to the lawyer a desire not to be solicited; or 2) the solicitation involves coercion, duress, or harassment. Model Rules of Prof'l Conduct R. 7.3(b).

b)   "Advertising Material"

Every written, recorded or electronic communication from a lawyer soliciting professional employment from anyone known to be in need of legal services in a particular matter must include the words "Advertising Material" on the outside envelope and at the beginning and ending of any recorded or electronic communication, unless the recipient of the communication is a lawyer or has a family, close personal, or prior professional relationship with the lawyer. Model Rules of Prof'l Conduct R. 7.3(c).

3)   SOLICITATION BY THIRD PARTIES

As a general principle, if the solicitation is carried out by a third party, it will be attributed to the lawyer if the elements of solicitation are otherwise present and the communication was directed by the lawyer.

C.   **Group Legal Services**

Notwithstanding the general prohibitions upon solicitation, a lawyer may participate in a prepaid or group legal service plan operated by an organization not owned or directed by the lawyer, even if that group uses in-person or telephone contact to solicit memberships or subscriptions for the plan. However, the group must not solicit memberships or subscriptions from people who are known to be in need of legal services in a particular matter covered by the plan. Model Rules of Prof'l Conduct R. 7.3(d).

★   D.   **Referrals**

1)   PAYMENT FOR RECOMMENDING A LAWYER'S SERVICES

A lawyer must not give anything of value to another person as payment for recommending the lawyer's services. Model Rules of Prof'l Conduct R. 7.2(b). This Rule is subject to the following exceptions:

a)   Reasonable Costs of Advertisements or Communications

A lawyer may pay the reasonable costs of advertisements or communications. Model Rules of Prof'l Conduct R. 7.2(b)(1).

b)   Legal Service Plans and Certain Lawyer Referral Services

A lawyer may pay the usual charges of a legal service plan or a not-for-profit or qualified lawyer referral service. Model Rules of Prof'l Conduct R. 7.2(b)(2). A qualified lawyer referral service is a lawyer referral service that has been approved by an appropriate regulatory agency. *Id.*

c)   Purchase of Law Practice

A lawyer can pay for a law practice that the lawyer acquires. Model Rules of Prof'l Conduct R. 7.2(b)(3).

d)   Reciprocal Referral Agreement

A lawyer can refer clients to another lawyer or a nonlawyer professional pursuant to an agreement (not otherwise prohibited by the Rules) providing for the other person to refer clients or customers to the lawyer if: 1) the reciprocal referral agreement is not exclusive; and 2) the client is informed of the agreement's existence and nature. Model Rules of Prof'l Conduct R. 7.2(b)(4).

E.   Communications of Fields of Practice and Specialization

1)   FIELDS OF PRACTICE

A lawyer may communicate the fact that the lawyer does or does not practice in particular fields of law. Model Rules of Prof'l Conduct R. 7.4(a).

a)   Patent Lawyers

A lawyer admitted to engage in patent practice before the United States Patent and Trademark Office may use the designation "Patent Attorney" or a substantially similar designation. Model Rules of Prof'l Conduct R. 7.4(b).

b)   Admiralty Lawyers

A lawyer engaged in Admiralty practice may use the designation "Admiralty," "Proctor in Admiralty," or a substantially similar designation. Model Rules of Prof'l Conduct R. 7.4(c).

2)   SPECIALIZATION

Generally, a lawyer is permitted to assert that the lawyer is a "specialist" in particular fields, but the assertion must not be "false and misleading." A lawyer must not state or imply that a lawyer is *certified* as a specialist in a particular field of law unless: 1) the lawyer has been certified as a specialist by an organization that has been approved by an appropriate state authority or accredited by the ABA; and 2) the name of the certifying organization is clearly identified in the communication. Model Rules of Prof'l Conduct R. 7.4(d).

COMMUNICATION ABOUT LEGAL SERVICES

REVIEW QUESTIONS

1. A lawyer is permitted to conduct limited advertising in public communications which may include:
   a. statements of fact or opinion that create unjustified expectations in potential clients or unfair comparisons to other lawyers.
   b. declarations of win, losses, or ties in court proceedings.
   c. statements declaring the lawyer's relationships with judges or other heads of tribunals or elected officials.
   d. statements of fact as to the attorney's name, business address, phone number, website, and hours.

2. A lawyer may make a written, recorded, or electronic communication advertisement to the public as long as the advertisement:
   a. contains the lawyer's name and office address, is kept for two years, and is produced on demand by regulatory authorities.
   b. declares the lawyer's expertise and mentions other clients who regularly are represented and rely upon that expertise.
   c. is preapproved by the regulatory authority so as to avoid potential liability.
   d. is filed with the regulatory authority at least five business days prior to publication and not found too libelous, slanderous, or false in any manner.

3. A lawyer cannot give anything of value to another person or entity for recommending their services, except:
   a. a business card.
   b. the reasonable costs of advertising or communications, the usual charge of a legal service plan or lawyer referral service approved by the state's legal regulatory agency, or the cost of a law practice the lawyer purchases.
   c. an invitation to the lawyer's or law firm's annual holiday dinner and party where gifts are anonymously exchanged by all attendees.
   d. a promise to give discounted rates based on future clients' referrals.

4. Reciprocal referral agreements (RRA) are:
   a. allowed if the RRA is exclusive.
   b. allowed if the client is informed of the existence and nature of the agreement and the agreement is not exclusive.
   c. never allowed.
   d. always allowed because to hold otherwise would restrain trade.

5. Solicitation by a lawyer is:
   a. permitted under all circumstances.
   b. prohibited if the lawyer's financial gain is the significant motivation.

c. prohibited unless the potential client is a lawyer or a close personal friend or a family member.

d. prohibited under all circumstances.

6. A lawyer's communications cannot state that a lawyer is a specialist unless:

a. the lawyer has undertaken continuing legal education for at least three years exclusively in the area of specialty and can provide proof of the same to the licensing authority that may grant such certification.

b. the lawyer is certified as such by at least one appointed judge who has observed the lawyer's practice, demeanor, knowledge, education, and experience before the court and determined that the lawyer has attained a proficient competency in the requisite specialty.

c. the lawyer is certified by the highest court in the state or federal judiciary with jurisdiction to hear such specialty cases.

d. the lawyer is certified as such by an organization approved by a state authority authorized to grant such certifications or by an ABA accredited agency, and the name of the certifying organization is clearly stated in the communication.

COMMUNICATION ABOUT LEGAL SERVICES

ANSWERS TO REVIEW QUESTIONS

Answer 1

The correct answer is choice D. A lawyer is permitted to conduct limited advertising in public communications which may include statements of fact as to the attorney's name, business address, phone number, website, and hours. However, the advertisement may not make statements of fact or opinion that create unjustified expectations in potential clients or unfair comparisons to other lawyers, declarations of wins, losses, or ties in court proceedings, or statements declaring the lawyer's relationships with judges or other heads of tribunals or elected officials.

Answer 2

The correct answer is choice A. A lawyer may make a written, recorded, or electronic communication advertisement to the public as long as the advertisement contains the lawyer's name and office address, is kept for two years, and is produced on demand by regulatory authorities.

Answer 3

The correct answer is choice B. A lawyer cannot give anything of value to another person or entity for recommending their services, except the reasonable costs of advertising or communications, the usual charge of a legal service plan or lawyer referral service approved by the state's legal regulatory agency, or the cost of a law practice they purchase.

Answer 4

The correct answer is choice B. Reciprocal referral agreements are allowed if the RRA is not exclusive and the client is informed of the existence and nature of the agreement.

Answer 5

The correct answer is choice C. Solicitation by a lawyer is prohibited unless the potential client is a lawyer or a close personal friend or a family member.

Answer 6

The correct answer is choice D. A lawyer's communications cannot state that a lawyer is a specialist unless the lawyer is certified as such by an organization approved by a state authority authorized to grant such certifications or by an ABA accredited agency, and the name of the certifying organization is clearly stated in the communication.

XI. LAWYERS' DUTIES TO THE PUBLIC AND THE LEGAL SYSTEM

A. Voluntary *Pro Bono* Service

Every lawyer has a professional responsibility to provide legal services to those unable to pay. A lawyer should aspire to render at least 50 hours of *pro bono publico* (i.e., free to the public) legal services per year. Model Rules of Prof'l Conduct R. 6.1.

1) SUBSTANTIAL MAJORITY OF SERVICES

In fulfilling this responsibility, the lawyer should provide a substantial majority of the 50 hours of legal services without fee or expectation of fee to persons of limited means or to charitable, religious, civic, community, governmental, and educational organizations in matters that are designed primarily to address the needs of persons of limited means. *Id.*

2) FOCUS OF VOLUNTARY SERVICE

In fulfilling this *pro bono* service responsibility, lawyers should provide legal services to:

- persons with limited means free of charge or at a substantially reduced fee; or
- participation in activities for improving the law, legal system, or legal profession; or
- charitable, religious, civic, governmental, and educational organizations free of charge or at a substantially reduced fee.

When a lawyer provides *pro bono* legal services to an organization, the lawyer's legal services and financial support should primarily aid the organization in addressing the needs of persons with limited means. The legal services could also further the group's organizational purposes if the payment of standard legal fees would significantly deplete the organization's economic resources.

B. Accepting Appointments

A lawyer must not seek to avoid appointment by a tribunal to represent a person except for good cause, such as:

- when representing the client is likely to result in violation of the Rules or other law;
- when representing the client is likely to result in an unreasonable financial burden on the lawyer; or
- if the client or the cause is so repugnant to the lawyer as to be likely to impair the client-lawyer relationship or the lawyer's ability to represent the client.

C. Serving in Legal Services Organizations

A lawyer may serve as a director, officer, or member of a legal services organization even if the organization serves people who have adverse interests to the lawyer's clients. However, the lawyer cannot knowingly participate in a decision or action of the organization if: 1) participating in the decision or action is incompatible with the lawyer's obligations to a client; or 2) the decision or action could have a materially adverse effect on the representation of a client of the organization whose interests are adverse to a client of the lawyer.

D. Law Reform Activities Affecting Client Interests

A lawyer may serve as a director, officer, or member of an organization involved in reform of the law even though the reform may affect the interests of a client of the lawyer. A lawyer serving in this capacity does not have a client-lawyer relationship with the organization. When the lawyer knows that a client's interests may be materially benefitted by a decision in which the lawyer participates, the lawyer must disclose the fact but does not need to identify the client.

E. Criticism of Judges and Adjudicating Officials

Lawyers contribute to improving the administration of justice by expressing their honest and candid opinions on the professional or personal fitness of persons being considered for election or appointment to judicial office. However, "a lawyer must not make a statement that the lawyer knows to be false or with reckless disregard as to its truth or falsity concerning the qualifications or integrity of a judge, adjudicatory officer, or candidate for election or appointment to judicial or legal office." Model Rules of Prof'l Conduct R. 8.2(a).

To maintain the fair and independent administration of justice, lawyers are encouraged to continue traditional efforts to defend judges and courts unjustly criticized.

F. Political Contributions to Obtain Engagements or Appointments

Lawyers have a right to participate fully in the political process, which includes making and soliciting political contributions to candidates for judicial and other public office. However, a lawyer or law firm must not accept a governmental legal engagement or an appointment by a judge if the lawyer or law firm makes a political contribution or solicits political contributions for the purpose of obtaining or being considered for that type of legal engagement or appointment.

1) POLITICAL CONTRIBUTION

The term "political contribution" means any gift, subscription, loan, advance, or deposit of anything of value made directly or indirectly to a candidate, incumbent, political party, or campaign committee to influence or provide financial support for election to or retention in judicial or other government office. Political contributions in initiative and referendum elections are not included. Furthermore, the term does not include any uncompensated services.

2) GOVERNMENT LEGAL ENGAGEMENT/JUDICIAL APPOINTMENT

The term "government legal engagement" means any engagement to provide legal services that a public official has the direct or indirect power to award. The term "appointment by a judge" means an appointment to a position such as referee, commissioner, special master, receiver, guardian, or other similar position that is made by a judge. However, these terms do not include:

- substantially uncompensated services;
- engagements or appointments made on the basis of experience, expertise, professional qualifications, and cost following a request for proposal or other process that is free from influence based upon political contributions; and
- engagements or appointments made on a rotational basis from a list compiled without regard to political contributions.

G. Improper Influence on Government Officials

It is professional misconduct for a lawyer to state or imply an ability to improperly influence a government agency or official.

H. Assisting Judicial Misconduct

It is professional misconduct for a lawyer to knowingly assist a judge or judicial officer in conduct that is a violation of applicable rules of judicial conduct or other law.

★★   ### I. Impropriety Incident to Public Service

1) LAWYERS AS JUDICIAL CANDIDATES

A lawyer who is a candidate for judicial office must comply with the applicable provisions of the Model Code of Judicial Conduct. Model Rules of Prof'l Conduct R. 8.2(b). Some of the Code's provisions are described in the next section of this outline.

DUTIES TO THE PUBLIC AND THE LEGAL SYSTEM

REVIEW QUESTIONS

1. A lawyer involved with an organization that is developing or reforming the law must:
   a. refrain from representing any client who may benefit or be harmed by the lawyer's actions.
   b. disclose to the organization that the lawyer has a client who may benefit from the activity.
   c. register as a lobbyist and disclose the same to all current and potential clients to allow them to decide if such actions are to their detriment or against their interests.
   d. avoid invalidating a law if such invalidation would have a negative impact or unintended consequence on other laws.

2. Lawyers who are declared judicial candidates:
   a. are not subject to the Model Code of Judicial Conduct, as they have not been sworn onto the bench.
   b. must disclose such candidacy to current and potential clients as appointment to the bench may force them to recuse themselves from further representation and hinder effective and consistent representation of the client.
   c. must not appear before the court for which they are a judicial candidate to avoid an appearance of impropriety.
   d. are subject to the Model Code of Judicial Conduct, even before they ascend to the bench.

3. Every lawyer has a professional responsibility to provide pro bono services and aspire to provide at least 50 hours of pro bono service to the public. A substantial majority of that time must go toward:
   a. those identified by the state bar association as eligible charitable or civic organizations or by the court as needy individuals.
   b. charitable contributions in lieu of pro bono hours as not all licensed attorneys are capable of providing legal representation.
   c. those unable to afford an attorney or to charitable or civic organizations addressing the needs of persons with limited means.
   d. pro bono service to government agencies in order to reduce the overall cost of public services, including legal services.

DUTIES TO THE PUBLIC AND THE LEGAL SYSTEM

ANSWERS TO REVIEW QUESTIONS

Answer 1

The correct answer is choice B. A lawyer involved with an organization that is developing or reforming a law must disclose to the organization that the lawyer has a client who may benefit from the activity.

Answer 2

The correct answer is choice D. Lawyers who are declared judicial candidates are subject to the Model Code of Judicial Conduct, even before they ascend to the bench.

Answer 3

The correct answer is choice C. A substantial majority of pro bono legal services must go toward those unable to afford an attorney or to charitable or civic organizations addressing the needs of persons with limited means.

★★★ XII. JUDICIAL CONDUCT

Judicial ethics are governed by the Model Code of Judicial Conduct's Canons and Rules.

A. Maintaining the Independence and Impartiality of the Judiciary

A judge must uphold and promote the independence, integrity, and impartiality of the judiciary. Model Code of Judicial Conduct Canon 1. A judge must avoid impropriety and the appearance of impropriety. *Id.* Moreover, a judge or candidate for judicial office must not engage in activity that is inconsistent with the judiciary's independence, integrity, and impartiality. Model Code of Judicial Conduct Canon 4.

1) COMPLIANCE WITH THE LAW

A judge must comply with the law. Model Code of Judicial Conduct Rule 1.1. Specifically, a judge or other judicial candidate in a public election must comply with all applicable laws and regulations concerning elections, campaigns, and fund raising. Model Code of Judicial Conduct Rule 4.2(A)(2).

2) PROMOTING CONFIDENCE IN THE JUDICIARY

A judge must act in a way that promotes public confidence in the judiciary's independence, integrity, and impartiality. Model Code of Judicial Conduct Rule 1.2.

a) Independence, Integrity, and Impartiality Defined

Independence means a judge's freedom from controls or influence beyond those set by law. Model Code of Judicial Conduct Terminology. Integrity means honesty, fairness, uprightness, and soundness of character. *Id.* "Impartially" or "impartial" means a lack of prejudice or bias in favor of, or against, specific parties or types of parties, as well as keeping an open mind when considering issues that could come before a judge. *Id.*

b) Avoiding Impropriety and the Appearance of Impropriety

A judge must avoid impropriety and the appearance of impropriety. Model Code of Judicial Conduct Rule 1.2. Actual improprieties include illegal conduct, conduct in violation of court rules, and conduct in violation of the Code. *Id.*, cmt. 5. Also, impropriety means conduct that undermines a judge's independence, integrity, or impartiality. Model Code of Judicial Conduct Terminology.

A judge's improper conduct (i.e., improprieties), as well as conduct that creates the appearance of impropriety, adversely affects public confidence in the judiciary. Model Code of Judicial Conduct Rule 1.2 cmt. 2. Because a judge is in the public eye, the judge should accept the Code's greater limitations upon conduct than those applicable to regular citizens, such as limits upon judicial speech. *Id.*

(1)   Test for Appearance of Impropriety

The appearance of impropriety exists when the judge's "conduct would create in reasonable minds a perception that the judge violated the Code or engaged in other conduct" that reflects negatively on the judge's impartiality, honesty, temperament, or fitness. Model Code of Judicial Conduct Rule 1.2 cmt. 5.

3)   AVOIDING ABUSE OF THE PRESTIGE OF JUDICIAL OFFICE

A judge must not abuse the prestige of judicial office in order to advance the personal or economic interests of the judge or others. Model Code of Judicial Conduct Rule 1.3. A judge must not allow others to abuse the prestige of judicial office in order to advance their personal or economic interests. *Id.*

a)   Improper Use of Judicial Office

A judge engages in improper conduct by attempting to use or using the judge's position to gain personal advantage or deferential treatment. *Id.*, cmt. 1. For example, a judge may not refer to the judge's official status in order to obtain favorable treatment in encounters with law enforcement officers. *Id.* Likewise, a judge cannot use official judicial letterhead to obtain an advantage in carrying on the judge's personal business affairs. *Id.* Generally, a judge can serve as a reference or provide a letter or recommendation for someone that the judge personally knows, provided that the judge complies with the above provisions. Model Code of Judicial Conduct Rule 1.3 cmt. 2.

B.   Performing the Duties of Judicial Office Impartially, Competently, and Diligently

A judge must perform the duties of judicial office impartially, competently, and diligently. Model Code of Judicial Conduct Canon 2.

1)   GIVING PRECEDENCE TO THE DUTIES OF JUDICIAL OFFICE

A judge's judicial duties take precedence over all the judge's other activities. Model Code of Judicial Conduct Rule 2.1. Judicial duties include all the duties of the judge's office prescribed by law. *Id.* In order to ensure that judges are available to do their judicial duties, they must conduct their extrajudicial and personal activities so as to reduce the risk of conflicts that would result in their disqualification from participation in proceedings. *Id.*, cmt. 1. Disqualification of judges is addressed later in this outline.

2)   IMPARTIALITY AND FAIRNESS

A judge must uphold and apply the law. Model Code of Judicial Conduct Rule 2.2. The judge must perform all judicial duties fairly and impartially. *Id.* In order to ensure fairness and impartiality, the judge must manifest objectivity and open-mindedness. *Id.*, cmt. 1. The judge must interpret and apply the law regardless of whether the judge approves of the law. Model Code of Judicial Conduct Rule 2.2 cmt. 2.

3) BIAS, PREJUDICE, AND HARASSMENT

a) Judges Must Perform Judicial Duties without Bias or Prejudice

A judge must perform judicial duties without bias or prejudice. Model Code of Judicial Conduct Rule 2.3(A). A judge who manifests bias or prejudice in a proceeding impairs the proceeding's fairness. *Id.*, cmt. 1.

b) Judges May Not Manifest Bias or Prejudice, or Harassment

A judge must not, in the performance of judicial duties, manifest bias or prejudice, or engage in harassment, including but not limited to bias, prejudice, or harassment based upon race, gender, sex, religion, ethnicity, national origin, disability, age, marital status, sexual orientation, political affiliation, or socioeconomic status. Model Code of Judicial Conduct Rule 2.3(B). A judge must not permit court officials, court staff, and others subject to the judge's direction and control to do so. *Id.* However, a judge may make legitimate references to the above factors if they are pertinent to an issue in a proceeding. Model Code of Judicial Conduct Rule 2.3(D).

c) Judges Must Require Lawyers to Refrain from Improper Conduct

A judge must require lawyers in proceedings before the judge to refrain from manifesting bias or prejudice, or engaging in harassment based upon race, gender, sex, religion, ethnicity, national origin, disability, age, marital status, sexual orientation, or socioeconomic status against parties, witnesses, counsel, or others. Model Code of Judicial Conduct Rule 2.3(C). However, lawyers may make legitimate references to those listed factors if they are pertinent to an issue in a proceeding. Model Code of Judicial Conduct Rule 2.3(D).

4) EXTERNAL INFLUENCES ON JUDICIAL CONDUCT

In order for an independent judiciary to exist, judges need to decide cases based on the law and facts, regardless of whether specific laws or parties to cases are unpopular or popular. Model Code of Judicial Conduct Rule 2.4 cmt. 1.

a) Public Clamor or Fear of Criticism May Not Sway Judges

A judge must not be swayed by public clamor or fear of criticism. Model Code of Judicial Conduct Rule 2.4(A).

b) Certain Relationships or Interests May Not Influence Judges

A judge must not allow family, social, financial, political, or other relationships or interests to influence the judge's judicial conduct or judgment. Model Code of Judicial Conduct Rule

2.4(B). For example, a judge cannot allow any relationship to affect the judge's impartiality in judicial decision-making.

c)   No Conveying that One Occupies Position to Influence Judges

A judge may not convey or allow others to convey the impression that any organization or person occupies a position to influence the judge. Model Code of Judicial Conduct Rule 2.4(C). For example, a judge should prevent a close friend from indicating that the friend can influence the judge.

5)   <u>COMPETENCE, DILIGENCE, AND COOPERATION</u>

a)   Requirements of Competence and Diligence

A judge must perform administrative and judicial duties competently and diligently. Model Code of Judicial Conduct Rule 2.5(A). "Competence in the performance of judicial duties requires the legal knowledge, skill, thoroughness, and preparation reasonably necessary to perform" a judge's judicial responsibilities. Model Code of Judicial Conduct Rule 2.5 cmt. 1. A judge should supervise and monitor cases in ways that eliminate or reduce dilatory practices, avoidable delays, and unnecessary costs. Model Code of Judicial Conduct Rule 2.5 cmt. 4.

b)   Requirement of Cooperation

The judge must cooperate with other judges and court officials in the administration of court business. Model Code of Judicial Conduct Rule 2.5(B).

6)   <u>ENSURING THE RIGHT TO BE HEARD</u>

The right of people to be heard in a court is a key aspect of a fair and impartial justice system. Model Code of Judicial Conduct Rule 2.6 cmt. 1. Observance of procedures protecting the right to be heard is necessary to protect a litigant's substantive rights. *Id.*

a)   Judge Must Provide the Right to Be Heard

A judge must provide every person who has a legal interest in a proceeding, or that person's lawyer, the right to be heard in the proceeding according to law. Model Code of Judicial Conduct Rule 2.6(A).

b)   Judge May Encourage Settlement of Disputed Matters

A judge may encourage parties to a proceeding and their lawyers to settle matters in dispute. Model Code of Judicial Conduct Rule 2.6(B). However, the judge may not act in a way that coerces any party into settlement of disputed matters. *Id.* Such improper conduct by the judge could undermine a party's legal right to be heard. Model Code of Judicial Conduct Rule 2.6 cmt. 2.

A judge should consider the effect that participation in settlement discussions can have on the judge's objectivity and impartiality and the appearance of judicial objectivity and impartiality. Model Code of Judicial Conduct Rule 2.6 cmt. 2.

7) RESPONSIBILITY TO DECIDE

A judge must hear and decide matters assigned to the judge, unless the Code or other law requires the judge's disqualification from the matter. Model Code of Judicial Conduct Rule 2.7. Disqualification may be required to protect the rights of litigants or to preserve public confidence in the judiciary's independence, integrity, and impartiality. *Id.*, cmt. 1. A judge should not use disqualification to avoid matters that involve difficult, unpopular, or controversial issues. *Id.* Disqualification of a judge is addressed later in this outline.

8) DECORUM, DEMEANOR, AND COMMUNICATION WITH JURORS

A judge must require order and decorum in proceedings before the judge. Model Code of Judicial Conduct Rule 2.8(A).

A judge must be patient, dignified, and courteous to jurors, litigants, witnesses, lawyers, court officials, court staff, and others with whom the judge deals in an official capacity. Model Code of Judicial Conduct Rule 2.8(B). The judge must require similar conduct of lawyers, court officials, court staff, and others subject to the judge's direction and control. *Id.*

9) JUDICIAL STATEMENTS ON IMPENDING AND PENDING CASES

Some restrictions on judicial speech are essential to the maintenance of the judiciary's independence, integrity, and impartiality. Model Code of Judicial Conduct Rule 2.10 cmt. 1.

a) Definition of Impending Matter and Pending Matter

An impending matter is one that is imminent or anticipated to occur soon, but has not yet begun. Model Code of Judicial Conduct Terminology. A pending matter is one that has begun, but has not yet reached final disposition. *Id.* A matter remains pending through any appellate process until its final disposition. *Id.*

b) Judge May Not Make Certain Types of Statements

While a matter is impending or pending in any court, a judge must not make any public statement that might reasonably be expected to impair its fairness or affect its outcome. Model Code of Judicial Conduct Rule 2.10(A). Also, the judge must not make any nonpublic statement that might substantially interfere with a fair trial or hearing. *Id.*

(1) Judge Must Require Others to Refrain from Statements

The judge must require that court staff, court officials, and others subject to the judge's direction and control refrain from making the foregoing types of prohibited statements. Model Code of Judicial Conduct Rule 2.10(C).

(2) Certain Exceptions Exist

A judge may make public statements in the course of the judge's official duties. Model Code of Judicial Conduct Rule 2.10(D). A judge may explain court procedures. *Id.* A judge may comment on a proceeding in which the judge is a litigant in a personal capacity. *Id.*

(3) Judge May Respond to Certain Types of Allegations

Subject to the foregoing rule's requirements about judges' statements, a judge may respond to allegations about the judge's conduct in a matter. Model Code of Judicial Conduct Rule 2.10(E). The judge may respond to such allegations directly or through a third party. *Id.*

c) What Judge May Not Say Regarding Anticipated Matters

A judge must not, with respect to cases, controversies, or issues that are likely to come before the court, make pledges, promises, or commitments that are inconsistent with the judge's impartial performance of adjudicative duties. Model Code of Judicial Conduct Rule 2.10(B).

The judge must require that court staff, court officials, and others subject to the judge's direction and control refrain from making the types of prohibited statements described above. Model Code of Judicial Conduct Rule 2.10(C).

10) SUPERVISORY DUTIES

a) Court Staff, Court Officials, and Others

A judge must require court staff, court officials, and others subject to the judge's direction and control to act in a way consistent with the judge's duties pursuant to the Code. Model Code of Judicial Conduct Rule 2.12(A).

b) Judge with Supervisory Authority

A judge with supervisory authority for the judicial performance of other judges must take reasonable measures to ensure that these judges properly perform their judicial responsibilities, including their prompt disposition of matters before them. Model Code of Judicial Conduct Rule 2.12(B).

11) ADMINISTRATIVE APPOINTMENTS

a) General Limitations on Judge's Power of Appointment

When a judge exercises the power to make administrative appointments, the judge must do this impartially and on the basis of merit. Model Code of Judicial Conduct Rule 2.13(A)(1).

A judge must avoid favoritism, nepotism, and unnecessary appointments. Model Code of Judicial Conduct Rule 2.13(A)(2).

b) Election Contribution Limit on Judge's Power of Appointment

A judge must not appoint a lawyer to a position if the judge either knows that the lawyer, or the lawyer's domestic partner or spouse, has contributed more than a specified dollar amount within the specified number of years prior to the judge's election campaign, or learns of such a contribution on account of a timely motion. Model Code of Judicial Conduct Rule 2.13(B).

(1) Exceptions to Limits on Judge's Appointments

Generally, the preceding limitation on a judge's power of appointment based on an election contribution applies, *unless*:

- the position is substantially uncompensated;
- the lawyer has been selected in rotation from a list of available and qualified lawyers compiled without regard to their having made political contributions; or
- the judge finds that no other lawyer is competent, willing, and able to accept the position. *Id.*

c) Judge May not Approve Compensation Greater than Fair Value

A judge must not approve compensation of appointees greater than the fair value of services rendered. Model Code of Judicial Conduct Rule 2.13(B).

12) DISABILITY AND IMPAIRMENT

a) When Judge Must Take Action about Impairment

A judge must take appropriate action when the judge has a reasonable belief that the performance of another judge or a lawyer is impaired by alcohol, drugs, or an emotional, mental, or physical condition. Model Code of Judicial Conduct Rule 2.14.

(1) What Constitutes Appropriate Action

Appropriate action may include a confidential referral to a lawyer or judicial assistance program. *Id.* "Appropriate action" means action intended and reasonably likely to assist the impaired judge or lawyer in handling the problem and prevent harm to the justice system. *Id.*, cmt. 1.

13) RESPONDING TO JUDICIAL AND LAWYER MISCONDUCT

a) Another Judge's Code Violation

A judge having knowledge that another judge has committed a violation of the Code that raises a substantial question about the other judge's trustworthiness, honesty, or fitness for judicial office must inform the appropriate authority. Model Code of Judicial Conduct Rule 2.15(A).

A judge who receives information indicating a substantial likelihood that another judge has committed a violation of the Code must take appropriate action. Model Code of Judicial Conduct Rule 2.15(C).

b) A Lawyer's Rules Violation

A judge having knowledge that a lawyer has committed a violation of the Rules that raises a substantial question as to the lawyer's trustworthiness, honesty, or fitness as a lawyer in other regards must inform the appropriate authority. Model Code of Judicial Conduct Rule 2.15(B).

A judge who receives information indicating a substantial likelihood that a lawyer has committed a violation of the Rules must take appropriate action. Model Code of Judicial Conduct Rule 2.15(D).

14) COOPERATION WITH DISCIPLINARY AUTHORITIES

a) Requirement of Judge's Cooperation

A judge must cooperate and be honest and candid with lawyer and judicial disciplinary agencies. Model Code of Judicial Conduct Rule 2.16(A).

b) Prohibition of Judge's Retaliation

A judge may not retaliate against a person known or suspected to have cooperated or assisted with an investigation of a lawyer or a judge. Model Code of Judicial Conduct Rule 2.16(B).

★★ C. Ex Parte Communications

An *ex parte* communication is a communication made to a judge for or by one party outside the presence of the other party. To the extent reasonably possible, communications with a judge must include all parties or their lawyers. Model Code of Judicial Conduct Rule 2.9 cmt. 1.

1) GENERALLY, NO EX PARTE COMMUNICATION BY JUDGE

Subject to certain exceptions, a judge must not initiate, permit, or consider *ex parte* communications, or consider other communications made to the judge outside the presence of the parties, regarding an impending or pending matter. Model Code of Judicial Conduct Rule 2.9(A).

a) Scope of General Prohibition on Ex Parte Communications

Generally, the foregoing rule against a judge's involvement with *ex parte* communications applies to such communications with people other than the proceeding's participants, such as law teachers and other attorneys. Model Code of Judicial Conduct Rule 2.9(A) cmt. 3. However, the judge may consult with ethics advisory committees and outside counsel about compliance with the Code. Model Code of Judicial Conduct Rule 2.9(A) cmt. 7.

b) When Judge May Engage in Ex Parte Communications

Certain exceptions to the general rule exist permitting specific *ex parte* communications:

(1) Scheduling, Administrative, or Emergency Purposes

When circumstances require it, *ex parte* communications for scheduling, administrative, or emergency purposes, which do not deal with substantive matters, are allowed, provided:

- No Procedural or Tactical Advantage

the judge reasonably believes that no party will gain a substantive, procedural, or tactical advantage as a result of the *ex parte* communication; and

- Notice and Opportunity to Respond

the judge makes provision promptly to notify all other parties of the substance of the *ex parte* communication, and affords the parties an opportunity to respond.

Model Code of Judicial Conduct Rule 2.9(A)(1).

★ ### (2) Disinterested Expert's Advice

A judge may obtain the written advice of a disinterested expert on the law applicable to a proceeding before the judge, if the judge: (1) notifies the parties of the person to be consulted and the subject matter of the advice to be procured; and (2) provides the parties a reasonable opportunity to object and respond to the notice and to the advice received. Model Code of Judicial Conduct Rule 2.9(A)(2).

(3) Court Officials, Court Staff, and Other Judges

Generally, a judge may consult with court officials and court staff whose functions are to assist the judge in conducting the judge's adjudicative responsibilities, or with other judges. Model Code of Judicial Conduct Rule 2.9(A)(3).

(a) Limits on Consultation with Other Judges

Although a judge may consult with another judge on a pending matter, the judge must avoid *ex parte* discussions about a case with other judges who have been disqualified from hearing it, and with judges who have appellate jurisdiction over it. *Id.*, cmt. 5.

(4)   Parties and their Lawyers

A judge may, with the consent of the parties, confer separately with the parties and their lawyers in an effort to mediate or settle matters pending before the judge. Model Code of Judicial Conduct Rule 2.9(A)(4).

(5)   Authorized by Law

A judge may initiate, permit, or consider any *ex parte* communications when expressly authorized by law to do so. Model Code of Judicial Conduct Rule 2.9(A)(5). For example, the judge may have such authority when serving on therapeutic or problem-solving courts, drug courts, or mental health courts. *Id.*, cmt. 4. In that capacity, the judge may have a more interactive role with parties, social workers, treatment providers, probation officers, and others. *Id.*

2)   INADVERTENT RECEIPT OF EX PARTE COMMUNICATION

If a judge inadvertently receives an unauthorized *ex parte* communication concerning the substance of a matter, then the judge must make provision promptly to notify the parties of the communication's substance and afford the parties with an opportunity to respond. Model Code of Judicial Conduct Rule 2.9(B).

3)   CANNOT INVESTIGATE AND IS LIMITED TO EVIDENCE/FACTS

A judge may not investigate facts in a matter independently. Model Code of Judicial Conduct Rule 2.9(C). The judge must consider only the evidence presented and those facts that may properly be judicially noticed. *Id.*

4)   ENSURE COMPLIANCE ABOUT EX PARTE COMMUNICATIONS

A judge must make reasonable efforts, including providing appropriate supervision, to ensure that the Code's provision regarding *ex parte* communications is not violated by court officials, court staff, and others subject to the judge's direction and control. Model Code of Judicial Conduct Rule 2.9(D).

★★★ **D.   Disqualification**

A judge has a duty to disqualify herself from any participation in a proceeding in which the judge's impartiality might reasonably be questioned. Model Code of Judicial Conduct Rule 2.11(A). This duty applies whether or not a party files a motion to disqualify the judge. *Id.*, cmt. 2.

1)   WHEN IMPARTIALITY MIGHT REASONABLY BE QUESTIONED

Generally, the Code requires disqualification in a proceeding in which the judge's impartiality might reasonably be questioned, regardless of whether any of the following specific provisions apply. *Id.*, cmt. 1. The judge's impartiality might reasonably be questioned in the following types of circumstances.

a) Personal Bias or Prejudice

Disqualification is required if the judge has a personal bias or prejudice regarding a party's lawyer or a party. Model Code of Judicial Conduct Rule 2.11(A)(1).

b) Personal Knowledge

Disqualification is required if the judge has personal knowledge of facts that are in dispute in the proceeding. *Id.*

★ ### c) Certain Types of Connections to Proceedings

Disqualification is required if the judge knows that the judge, the judge's domestic partner/spouse, or a person within a third degree of relationship to either of them, or the domestic partner or spouse of such a person is:

- a party to the proceeding, or an officer, director, managing member, general partner, or trustee of a party;
- a lawyer in the proceeding;
- a person who has more than a *de minimis* interest that could be substantially affected by the proceeding; or
- likely to be a material witness in the proceeding.

Model Code of Judicial Conduct Rule 2.11(A)(2).

★ ### d) Economic Interests

Disqualification is required if the judge knows that the judge, individually or as a fiduciary, or the judge's domestic partner, spouse, parent, or child, or any other member of the judge's family residing in the judge's household, has an economic interest in the subject matter in controversy or in a party to the proceeding. Model Code of Judicial Conduct Rule 2.11(A)(3).

(1) De Minimis Interest

Generally, an economic interest means ownership of more than a *de minimis* equitable or legal interest. Model Code of Judicial Conduct Terminology. In the context of interests regarding a judge's disqualification, "*de minimus*" means a minor interest that could not present a reasonable question about the judge's impartiality. *Id.*

e) Contributions to Judge's Campaign

Disqualification is required when the judge learns or knows by means of a timely motion that a party's lawyer, a party, or the party's lawyer's law firm has, within the prior certain number of years, made contributions to the judge's campaign in an amount that is more than a specified dollar amount. Model Code of Judicial Conduct Rule 2.11(A)(4).

f) Statement by Judge Regarding Issue

Disqualification is required if the judge has made a public statement that commits, or appears to commit, the judge to rule in a specific way or to reach a specific result in the proceeding or controversy. Model Code of Judicial Conduct Rule 2.11(A)(5). This rule does not apply to such a public statement made in a court proceeding, judicial opinion, or decision. *Id.*

★ ### g) Judge Served as Lawyer

Disqualification is required if the judge served as a lawyer in the matter. Model Code of Judicial Conduct Rule 2.11(A)(6)(a).

h) Judge was Associated with Lawyer

Disqualification is required if the judge was associated with a lawyer who participated substantially in the matter during that association. *Id.*

i) Judge Served in Governmental Employment

Disqualification is required if the judge served in governmental employment and in this capacity participated substantially and personally as a public official or lawyer regarding the proceeding. Model Code of Judicial Conduct Rule 2.11(A)(6)(b). The judge must also be disqualified if the judge served in governmental employment and publicly expressed in that capacity an opinion regarding the merits of the matter in controversy. *Id.*

j) Judge Served as Material Witness

Disqualification is required if the judge served as a material witness concerning the matter. Model Code of Judicial Conduct Rule 2.11(A)(6)(c).

k) Judge Presided as Judge

Disqualification is required if the judge previously presided as a judge over the matter in another court. Model Code of Judicial Conduct Rule 2.11(A)(6)(d).

★ ### 2) JUDGE'S PERSONAL AND FIDUCIARY ECONOMIC INTERESTS

A judge must keep informed regarding the judge's personal and fiduciary economic interests. Model Code of Judicial Conduct Rule 2.11(B). Also, the judge must make a reasonable effort to keep informed about the personal economic interests of the judge's domestic partner or spouse and minor children residing in the judge's household. *Id.*

★ ### 3) WAIVER OF DISQUALIFICATION

A judge subject to disqualification pursuant to the Code, other than for bias or prejudice, may disclose the basis of the judge's disqualification and may ask the parties and their lawyers to consider, outside the presence of court personnel and the judge, whether to waive disqualification. Model Code of Judicial Conduct Rule 2.11(C). If, after the disclosure, the lawyers and parties agree, without participation by court personnel and the judge, that the judge should not be disqualified, then the judge may participate in the proceeding. *Id.*

4) NECESSITY MAY OVERRIDE DISQUALIFICATION

This general rule of disqualification is subject to exceptions in case law and in the Code:

> The rule of necessity may override the rule of disqualification. For example, a judge might be required to participate in judicial review of a judicial salary statute, or might be the only judge available in a matter requiring immediate judicial action, such as a hearing on probable cause or a temporary restraining order.

Model Code of Judicial Conduct Rule 2.11 cmt. 3.

E. Extrajudicial Activities

A judge must conduct personal and extrajudicial activities so as to minimize the risk of conflict with judicial obligations. Model Code of Judicial Conduct Canon 3.

Extrajudicial activities include certain types of conduct by the judge that occurs outside of the judge's judicial office. Several Code provisions fall under this category.

1) LIMITATIONS ON JUDGE'S EXTRAJUDICIAL ACTIVITIES

A judge may participate in extrajudicial activities, other than those prohibited by law or the Code. Model Code of Judicial Conduct Rule 3.1.

a) Interfering with Proper Performance of Judicial Duties

A judge must not participate in extrajudicial activities that will interfere with the proper performance of the judge's judicial duties. Model Code of Judicial Conduct Rule 3.1(A).

b) Leading to Frequent Disqualification

A judge must not participate in extrajudicial activities that will lead to frequent disqualification of the judge. Model Code of Judicial Conduct Rule 3.1(B).

c) Undermining Independence, Integrity, or Impartiality

A judge must not participate in extrajudicial activities that would appear to a reasonable person to undermine the judge's independence, integrity, or impartiality. Model Code of Judicial Conduct Rule 3.1(C).

(1)   Discriminatory Conduct; Expressions of Prejudice or Bias

Discriminatory conduct and expressions of prejudice or bias by a judge, even outside the judge's judicial or official actions, are likely to appear to a reasonable person to call into question the judge's impartiality and integrity. *Id.*, cmt. 3. Examples include remarks or jokes that demean individuals based upon their gender, sex, race, religion, ethnicity, national origin, age, disability, sexual orientation, or socioeconomic status. *Id.*

d)   Appearing to be Coercive

When participating in extrajudicial activities, a judge may not engage in conduct that would appear to a reasonable person to be coercive. Model Code of Judicial Conduct Rule 3.1(D).

e)   Using Court Resources

When engaging in extrajudicial activities, a judge must not make use of court staff, premises, equipment, stationery, or other resources, except for incidental use for activities that concern the legal system, the law, or the administration of justice, or unless the law allows such additional use. Model Code of Judicial Conduct Rule 3.1(E).

2)   APPEARANCES BEFORE GOVERNMENTAL BODIES AND CONSULTATION WITH GOVERNMENT OFFICIALS

a)   Generally, No Appearances at Public Hearings or Consultation

As a general rule, a judge must not appear voluntarily at a public hearing before, or otherwise consult with, an executive or legislative body or official except:

- on matters concerning the law, the legal system, or the administration of justice;
- on matters about which the judge obtained expertise or knowledge during the judge's official duties; or
- when acting *pro se* in a matter involving the judge's economic or legal interests, or when the judge is acting as a fiduciary.

Model Code of Judicial Conduct Rule 3.2.

3)   APPOINTMENTS TO GOVERNMENTAL POSITIONS

A judge must not accept appointment to a governmental committee, commission, board, or other governmental position unless the position concerns the law, the legal system, or the administration of justice. Model Code of Judicial Conduct Rule 3.4.

For example, a judge may not serve on the board of a public educational institution, unless the institution is a law school. However, service on the board of a public law school or any private educational institution would usually be permitted.

4) TESTIFYING AS CHARACTER WITNESS

Except when a judge is duly summoned, a judge must not testify as a character witness in an administrative, judicial, or other adjudicatory proceeding or otherwise vouch for the character of a person in a legal proceeding. Model Code of Judicial Conduct Rule 3.3.

a) Abuse of Prestige of Office by Testifying as Character Witness

If a judge testifies as a character witness without being subpoenaed to testify, then the judge abuses the prestige of judicial office in order to advance someone else's interests. *Id.*, cmt. 1.

5) USE OF NONPUBLIC INFORMATION

A judge must not intentionally disclose or use, for any purpose unrelated to the judge's judicial duties, nonpublic information acquired in a judicial capacity. Model Code of Judicial Conduct Rule 3.5. This is not intended to affect a judge's ability to act on information as necessary to protect the safety or health of a judge, a member of the judge's family, other judicial officers, or court personnel if consistent with the Code's other provisions. *Id.*, cmt. 2.

6) AFFILIATION WITH DISCRIMINATORY ORGANIZATIONS

A judge may not hold membership in an organization that engages in invidious discrimination on the grounds of race, gender, sex, religion, ethnicity, national origin, or sexual orientation. Model Code of Judicial Conduct Rule 3.6(A). Moreover, a judge cannot use the benefits or facilities of an organization if the judge knows, or should know, that the organization engages in invidious discrimination. However, a judge may attend an event in a facility of such an organization when the judge's attendance is an isolated event that could not reasonably be perceived as an endorsement of the organization's practices. Model Code of Judicial Conduct Rule 3.6(B)

a) Prohibited Membership Gives Appearance of Impropriety

A judge's membership in an organization that engages in invidious discrimination gives rise to perceptions "that the judge's impartiality is impaired." *Id.*, cmt. 1. This issue relates to matters of federal constitutional law.

A judge must resign immediately from an organization upon learning that the organization engages in invidious discrimination. Model Code of Judicial Conduct Rule 3.6 cmt. 3.

7) PARTICIPATION IN EDUCATIONAL, RELIGIOUS, CHARITABLE, FRATERNAL, OR CIVIC ORGANIZATIONS AND ACTIVITIES

Generally, judges may engage in non-profit educational, religious, charitable, fraternal, or civic extrajudicial activities, even when those activities do not involve the law. Model Code of Judicial Conduct Rule 3.1 cmt. 1 (20).

a) Activities Sponsored by Organizations or Governmental Entities

Generally, subject to the other, earlier addressed limitations upon a judge's participation in extrajudicial activities, a judge may engage in activities sponsored by organizations or governmental entities concerned with the law, the legal system, or the administration of justice. Model Code of Judicial Conduct Rule 3.7.

b) Activities of Non-Profit Organizations

Generally, subject to the other, earlier addressed limitations upon a judge's participation in extrajudicial activities, a judge may engage in activities of non-profit educational, religious, charitable, fraternal, or civic organizations.

c) Judge Can Participate in Activities of Organizations or Entities

Generally, relative to the foregoing types of organizations or entities, a judge may participate in activities such as these:

- soliciting contributions only from members of the judge's family, or from judges over whom the judge lacks authority;
- soliciting membership, but only if the organization or entity is concerned with the law, the legal system, or the administration of justice;
- participating in an event of an organization or entity that serves a fund-raising purpose, but only if the event concerns the law, the legal system, or the administration of justice;
- serving as an officer, director, trustee, or advisor of an entity, unless it is likely that the organization or entity will be engaged in proceedings before the judge or the court of which the judge is a member, or another court under its appellate jurisdiction.

Model Code of Judicial Conduct Rule 3.7(A)(2)-(4), (6).

8) APPOINTMENTS TO FIDUCIARY POSITIONS

a) Fiduciary for Family Member under Limited Circumstances

Usually, a judge may not accept appointment to serve in a fiduciary position. Model Code of Judicial Conduct Rule 3.8(A). However, an exception to this prohibition applies for the estate, trust, or person of the judge's family, and then only when such service will not interfere with the proper performance of judicial duties. *Id.* A fiduciary position includes executor, administrator, trustee, guardian, attorney in fact, or other personal representative. *Id.*

b)   When Judge May Not Serve as Fiduciary

A judge may not serve in a fiduciary position if the judge as fiduciary will likely be involved in proceedings that would normally come before the judge. Model Code of Judicial Conduct Rule 3.8(B). Alternatively, a judge may not serve in a fiduciary position if the trust, estate, or ward becomes involved in adversary proceedings in the court on which the judge serves, or another court under its appellate jurisdiction. *Id.*

9)   SERVICE AS ARBITRATOR OR MEDIATOR

Unless expressly authorized by law, a judge may not act as an arbitrator or a mediator or perform other judicial functions separate from the judge's official duties. Model Code of Judicial Conduct Rule 3.9(C). However, a judge may participate in arbitration, mediation, or settlement conferences conducted as part of assigned judicial duties. *Id.*, cmt. 1.

10)   PRACTICE OF LAW

A judge may not practice law. Model Code of Judicial Conduct Rule 3.10. A judge may not serve as a lawyer, even to represent a member of the judge's family. *Id.* However, the judge may act *pro se* by representing himself. *Id.* Also, the judge may, without compensation, provide legal advice to, and draft or review documents for, a member of the judge's family. *Id.*

11)   FINANCIAL, BUSINESS, OR REMUNERATIVE ACTIVITIES

a)   Permitted Financial Activities

★   (1)   Holding and Managing Investments

Generally, a judge may hold and manage the judge's investments and those of the judge's family members. Model Code of Judicial Conduct Rule 3.11(A).

(2)   Serving in Certain Capacities in Business Entities

Generally, a judge may not serve as a director, officer, manager, general partner, employee, or advisor of any business entity. Model Code of Judicial Conduct Rule 3.11(B). However, a judge may participate in or manage: 1) a business closely held by the judge or members of the judge's family; or 2) a business entity mainly involved in investment of the judge's financial resources and those of the judge's family members. *Id.*

b)   When a Judge May Not Engage in Permitted Financial Activities

A judge may not hold and manage investments or participate in or manage certain business entities if such activity will:

- interfere with proper performance of judicial duties;
- lead to the judge's frequent disqualification;

- "involve the judge in frequent transactions or continuing business relationships with lawyers or other persons likely to come before the court on which the judge serves"; or
- result in other violations of the Code.

Model Code of Judicial Conduct Rule 3.11(C).

12) COMPENSATION FOR EXTRAJUDICIAL ACTIVITIES

Generally, a judge may accept reasonable compensation for extrajudicial activities allowed by the Code or other law. Model Code of Judicial Conduct Rule 3.12. However, the judge may not accept such compensation if this acceptance "would appear to a reasonable person to undermine the judge's independence, integrity, or impartiality." *Id.*

13) ACCEPTANCE AND REPORTING OF GIFTS, LOANS, BEQUESTS, BENEFITS, OR OTHER THINGS OF VALUE

If a judge accepts something of value, such as a gift, without paying fair market value for it, then a risk exists that a reasonable person could view it as intended to influence the judge's decision in some case. Model Code of Judicial Conduct Rule 3.13 cmt. 1. The following limitations are placed upon a judge's acceptance of certain things of value according to the degree of the risk that the acceptance would appear to undermine the judge's independence, integrity, or impartiality. *Id.*

a) When Judge Must Not Accept Something of Value

Generally, a judge must not accept a gift, loan, bequest, benefit, or other thing of value "if acceptance is prohibited by law or would appear to a reasonable person to undermine the judge's independence, integrity, or impartiality." Model Code of Judicial Conduct Rule 3.13(A).

b) When Judge May Accept Something of Value without Reporting It

Unless otherwise prohibited, a judge may accept certain types of items without publicly reporting such acceptance.

★   (1)   Items with Little Intrinsic Value

A judge may accept items with little intrinsic value, such as certificates, plaques, greeting cards, and trophies.

(2)   Things from Those for Whom Disqualification is Required

A judge may accept gifts, loans, bequests, benefits, or other things of value from relatives, friends, or other persons, including lawyers, whose interest or appearance in a proceeding impending or pending before the judge would require the judge's disqualification.

117

(3)   Ordinary Social Hospitality

A judge may accept ordinary social hospitality, such as an invitation to a festive party for a special occasion.

★   (4)   Financial or Commercial Opportunities and Benefits

A judge may accept financial or commercial benefits and opportunities, if the same benefits and opportunities or loans are made available on identical terms to people other than judges.

(5)   Prizes and Rewards Given in Public Contests

A judge may accept prizes and rewards given to participants or competitors in random contests, drawings, or other events that are open to people other than judges.

(6)   Fellowships, Scholarships, and Similar Items

A judge may accept fellowships, scholarships, and similar benefits and awards.

(7)   Resource Materials Provided by Publishers

A judge may accept resource materials provided by publishers for free and for official use (e.g., magazines, journals, books, audiovisual materials).

(8)   Awards, Gifts, or Benefits

A judge may accept awards, gifts, or benefits associated with the profession, business, or other separate activity of a domestic partner, spouse, or other family member of a judge living in the judge's household that incidentally benefit the judge.

Model Code of Judicial Conduct Rule 3.13(B)(1)-(8).

c)   When Judge May Accept Things of Value with Reporting

Unless otherwise prohibited, a judge may accept certain additional types of items, but the judge must publicly report their acceptance:

★   (1)   Gifts Incident to Public Testimonial

A judge must report accepted "gifts incident to a public testimonial";

(2)   Invitations for Free Attendance of Certain Events

A judge must report accepted invitations to a judge and the judge's domestic partner, spouse, or guest to attend without charge: 1) an event related to a bar-related function or another activity regarding the law, the legal system, or the administration of justice; or 2) an event connected with any of the judge's charitable, educational, fraternal, religious, or civic activities, if the identical invitation is given to non-judges who are involved in similar ways in the same activity; and

(3)   Things of Value from Certain Types of Parties or Attorneys

A judge must report accepted gifts, loans, bequests, benefits, or other things of value, if their source is a party or an attorney who has appeared or is likely to appear before the judge in a court, or whose interests have or could come before the judge in a court. Model Code of Judicial Conduct Rule 3.13(C)(1)-(3).

14)   REIMBURSEMENT OF EXPENSES, WAIVERS OF FEES/CHARGES

a)   General Considerations about Certain Reimbursement/Waiver

A judge may participate in permissible extrajudicial activity, such as attending a legal educational program sponsored by an educational, civic, fraternal, religious, or charitable organization. Model Code of Judicial Conduct Rule 3.14 cmt. 1.

b)   When Judge May Accept Certain Reimbursements/Waivers

Unless otherwise prohibited, a judge may accept reimbursement of reasonable and necessary expenses for food, travel, lodging, or other incidental expenses, or a waiver of fees or charges for registration, tuition, and similar items, from sources besides the judge's employer, if the expenses or charges are connected with the judge's participation in permissible extrajudicial activities. Model Code of Judicial Conduct Rule 3.14(A).

(1)   Limitation on Permissible Reimbursement

Reimbursement of a judge's expenses for necessary food, travel, lodging, or other incidental expenses is limited to the actual costs reasonably incurred by the judge and, when suitable to the occasion, by the judge's domestic partner, spouse, or guest. *Id.* Model Code of Judicial Conduct Rule 3.14(B).

c)   Public Reporting Requirement

A judge who accepts reimbursement of expenses or waivers of fees or charges on behalf of the judge or the judge's domestic partner, spouse, or guest must publicly report such acceptance. Model Code of Judicial Conduct Rule 3.14(C).

15)   PUBLIC REPORTING REQUIREMENTS

Generally, a judge must publicly report the amount of certain permissible reimbursements and other things of value received by the judge.

a)   Public Documents

The judge files a report in order to make it public. The judge must file the report as a public document in the court on which the judge serves or another office designated by law. Model Code of Judicial Conduct Rule 3.15(D).

b) Public Report Contents

If public reporting is required, then a judge must report:

- the description of any gift, loan, bequest, benefit, or other thing of value accepted;
- the activity for which the judge received any compensation; and
- the source of reimbursement of expenses or waiver of fees or charges.

Model Code of Judicial Conduct Rule 3.15(B).

c) Timing of Public Report

A judge must make a required public report at least annually. Model Code of Judicial Conduct Rule 3.15(C). However, a judge must make a required public report about reimbursement of expenses or waiver of fees or charges within 30 days after the end of the event or program for which the judge received such reimbursement or waiver.

d) What Must Be Publicly Reported

A judge must publicly report the amount or value of:

- compensation received by the judge for permissible extrajudicial activities;
- permissible gifts and other things of value received by a judge, unless their value does not exceed a specified dollar amount; and
- permissible reimbursement of expenses and waiver of fees or charges, unless it does not exceed a specified dollar amount.

Model Code of Judicial Conduct Rule 3.15(A)(3).

JUDICIAL CONDUCT

REVIEW QUESTIONS

1. The Model Code of Judicial Conduct's first canon requires a judge to uphold and promote the judiciary's:
    a. independence, integrity, and impartiality.
    b. independence, trustworthiness, and compliance with the law.
    c. honesty, trustworthiness, and impartiality.
    d. compliance with the law.

2. When a judge acts impartially, the judge has:
    a. no opinion on a case or controversy before the court.
    b. no feelings for, against, or in any manner, toward the parties or their attorneys.
    c. a lack of prejudice or bias in favor of, or against a party, as well as an open mind about all issues that come before the court.
    d. a respectful understanding of personal biases and prejudices and an ability to control them in any case or controversy.

3. "Impropriety" means:
    a. only violations of the law
    b. any speech that may offend
    c. any conduct that adversely affects public confidence in the judiciary
    d. decisions that embarrass other public officials

4. Whether a judge's conduct creates an appearance of impropriety is determined by:
    a. a judicial ethics panel composed of attorneys and judges.
    b. whether a reasonable person would perceive the judge to have violated the Code or otherwise acted in a manner that reflects negatively on the judge's impartiality, temperament, honesty, or fitness.
    c. a preponderance of the evidence submitted to the appropriate review authority.
    d. the state Supreme Court acting in its oversight and regulatory capacity of the judiciary.

5. If a judge's father-in-law attempts to impress and influence others with the judge's position, the judge must:
    a. advise court security officers to bring the father-in-law before the court to be formally notified that such conduct constitutes contempt of court and is an actionable offense.

      b. notify law enforcement officers that the father-in-law is interfering with court operations, which is an actionable offense.

      c. take reasonable action to not allow the father-in-law to abuse the prestige of judicial office in order to advance personal or economic interests.

      d. direct the judge's spouse to exercise all necessary control over the spouse's father to prevent detracting from the prestige of the judge and the court.

6. Which of the following is not an example of abuse of the prestige of judicial office:

      a. purchasing an expensive set of used leather office furniture for your chambers, posted for sale by a retiring partner of a local law firm

      b. mentioning your position as a judge to the tax appraisal official inspecting your new house.

      c. replying on official letterhead to several publishers who expressed interest in publishing your spouse's memoirs.

      d. having the title "Judge of the Superior Court" printed above your name on your personal stationary.

7. By accepting the position of judicial office, an individual:

      a. must withdraw from any other business, financial, or other opportunity that could present a conflict of interest before the court.

      b. gives up the right to participate in any other aspect of governmental activity that might lead to a conflict of interest or disqualification from a case or controversy.

      c. must advise family members and close friends not to engage in any activity which may compromise the integrity, honor, and impartiality of the judicial office by association.

      d. must conduct any extrajudicial and personal activities so as to reduce the risk of conflict or disqualification.

8. If a judge disapproves of a law that comes before the court, the judge must:

      a. notify all parties to the proceeding of the predisposition and consider any reasonable objection and request recusal from counsel.

      b. be automatically recused from the case to avoid any appearance of impropriety.

      c. interpret and apply the law regardless of any personal feelings, and the judge must manifest objectivity and open-mindedness in doing so.

      d. keep personal views private and rule as the judge believes to be proper.

9. Judge Martin, while listening to testimony in a civil rights case tried to a jury, was concerned about the derogatory language being used by multiple witnesses in the case. The Judge stopped the proceedings abruptly. In open court, the Judge banned the further use of twelve sexual, ethnic, and sexual orientation terms that were generally found

offensive and derogatory. Despite having heard the terms used by witnesses, several jurors were appalled that the Judge used such language and asked to be dismissed from jury duty. Judge Martin:

    a. displayed poor judgment and taste by repeating the derogatory language from the bench and is subject to sanction.

    b. demonstrated bias and prejudice by using such terms when the judge knew or should have known they would be offensive to jurors and, therefore, is subject to sanction.

    c. is not precluded from making legitimate references to factors such as sex, ethnicity, marital status, and sexual orientation when they are pertinent to an issue in the case.

    d. violated the Code by allowing others in court to use offensive language.

10. The juvenile court judge recently hired a clerk who is a 69-year-old woman who served in the same position in a local probate court for many years. The law clerk is generally quiet, but has demonstrated little tolerance for loud or poorly dressed adolescents. The juvenile court judge:

    a. should remind the new clerk that adolescents are going to challenge rules and conformity.

    b. should direct the new clerk that the clerk is held to the judicial standard of not manifesting bias or prejudice based on age or socioeconomic status.

    c. must fire the clerk for discrimination.

    d. should advise all adolescents in the court to maintain a respectful tone of voice and to dress respectfully when coming to court.

11. Judge Martin lives next door to a religious school and, although not affiliated with the religion, the judge's spouse is the school administrator. A highly charged and publicized case has come before the court asking the judge to decide if religious schools should be entitled to select state educational funding. Teachers from the religious school are picketing in front of the courthouse, and several parents of students have approached the judge's spouse to express their positions and question whether the spouse can adequately perform school duties if the judge does not decide the case "properly." Under the Code:

    a. the judge's spouse subjects the judge to undue influence and, therefore, the judge must be recused from the case.

    b. the judge cannot allow either public clamor or fear of criticism, or any family relationship or interest, to influence judicial judgment.

    c. the judge and the judge's spouse must be screened from each other while the case is pending.

    d. the judge must instruct the judge's spouse to inform anyone attempting to influence the spouse that such attempts are a violation of the Code under which they may be prosecuted.

12. The youngest judge to be appointed to the circuit court bench is also one of the most eligible single professionals according to the local newspaper. As a lawyer, the judge dated frequently and has previously indicated that the judge does not believe in marriage. Performing marriage ceremonies and presiding over divorces are now part of the judge's duties. The judge:
    a. must not allow social or other relationships or interests to influence judicial conduct or judgment.
    b. should be disqualified from performing marriage ceremonies and presiding over divorces.
    c. must be disqualified from performing marriage ceremonies and presiding over divorces.
    d. so as to avoid the appearance of bias, prejudice, or harassment based on marital status, the judge must publically proclaim the intent to accommodate the various views of marriage that others who may appear before the judge in court will espouse.

13. A judge has just been appointed to the bench. The judge's two children attend a private religious school that requires all parents to devote at least 16 hours each semester to religious-based public service work. The judge must:
    a. inform the school that the judge may be limited in availability to perform certain religious-based public service work as the judge must conduct extrajudicial and personal activities so as to reduce the risk of conflicts that would result in disqualification from participating in proceedings.
    b. decline the appointment if the judge intends to continue to perform the religious-based public service work as it is a conflict that will inevitably result in the judge's disqualification from proceedings.
    c. refuse to perform the religious-based public service work, even if it means the children will not be allowed to attend the school, as the judge's obligation to support the Constitution and laws require keeping a clear separation of church and state activities.
    d. find another school for the children if the school refuses to excuse the judge from service that could present the appearance of impropriety in favoring one religion over another.

14. A judge is the chief judge of the local circuit and has extensive administrative responsibilities. The judge's newest staff member, Steven, is married to the judge's niece. Steven does not demonstrate the cooperative spirit modeled by the judge and has demonstrated a temper to several attorneys. The judge has ignored repeated verbal

complaints about Steven, who has failed to properly maintain several active court files in the last month. Steven's actions are responsible for delays in several criminal hearings over the last two months. Steven also appears to have lost several court files that required costly replication by attorneys and the court. Morale among court staff is deteriorating, but the judge refuses to take action. The judge:

    a. has not violated the Code as personnel matters are within the discretion of the Chief Judge and fall outside of the Code's purview.

    b. has not violated the Code, which is designed to address professional legal problems.

    c. has violated the Code by not performing administrative duties competently and diligently, causing avoidable delays and unnecessary costs.

    d. has violated the Code by not cooperating with attorneys who rely on the judge's ability to administer the court effectively.

15. A judge believes that the parties in a divorce action are making unreasonable demands and acting openly hostile toward each other. The parties could only agree that they both trust the judge to hear their discrete matters relating to the divorce. The judge proposes to the attorneys to offer the parties a single opportunity to settle matters in the judge's chambers. If the parties could not reach an agreement, the judge would consider a motion to transfer the case to another judge for a hearing. The judge:

    a. violated the Code by coercing the parties should they not reach a settlement.

    b. violated the Code by denying the parties the right to be heard in a fair and impartial hearing.

    c. did not violate the Code because the judge was using the position to conserve judicial resources.

    d. did not violate the Code because the judge did not coerce any party into settlement of a disputed manner but, rather, considered the effect that participation in a settlement discussion may have on the judge's objectivity and impartiality.

16. A judge does not like publicity and attempts to avoid it if possible. A controversial adoption case, in which the prospective adoptive parents are both female, comes before the court. The judge elects to be disqualified from the case on "personal" grounds. The judge:

    a. does not have to hear and decide matters that cause personal angst. The judge's action does not violate the Code.

    b. must hear the case unless the Code or other law requires the judge's disqualification from the matter.

    c. does not have to hear the case if doing so may bring the judge's personal opinions and views into the public light and bring undue attention to the court and the parties.

    d. must hear the case because disqualification, without further explanation, brings the integrity of the entire judiciary into question.

17. A particular witness for the defendant in a bench trial is using vulgar language in answering questions on direct examination. The prosecutor objects to the use of such language. Defense counsel insists that the language is an important aspect of defense strategy and is an accurate representation of events surrounding the crime. Defense counsel also argues that, as this is a bench trial, no jurors are being offended. The judge should:

    a. overrule the objection because a judge cannot dictate defense strategy.

    b. overrule the objection because the judge can direct the witness to choose language more carefully.

    c. sustain the objection because court order and decorum must be maintained regardless of whether the proceeding is before a judge or jury.

    d. sustain the objection because the trial is open to the public and anyone, including minors, may enter the courtroom and be offended to hear such language in a court of law.

18. A resident alien is accused of making terroristic threats against government officials. Despite being told to do so by the bailiff, the defendant and the defendant's family members refuse to rise to their feet when the judge enters or exits the courtroom. Some jurors, court staff, and visitors are visibly offended by these actions. The judge:

    a. must require all persons before the court to demonstrate respect in accordance with the customs and traditions of the American judicial system.

    b. should advise defense counsel privately that the defendant's actions and the actions of friends, family, and supporters are disrespectful, disruptive, and may result in sanctions.

    c. must inform the protesters in open court that their actions are disruptive and will result in sanctions if they continue.

    d. must show patience, dignity, and courtesy to the defendant and others in the court who, while not abiding by custom or showing respect to the court, are not disrupting proceedings or the court by their actions.

19. A case with serious political implications is before a judge. Among themselves, the court staff has expressed strong opinions on both sides of the issue. The judge is aware of several comments made by the staffers. The judge must:

    a. admonish court staff to only make such statements outside of the courthouse and never to the parties, their attorneys, or to declared witnesses.

    b. not substantially interfere with the constitutional rights of citizens who are not judges to engage in free speech just because they are employed in the judicial branch of government.

    c. admonish court staff to not make statements, even nonpublic ones, that might substantially interfere with a fair trial or hearing, even though such admonishment may restrict speech.

    d. remind court staff that their comments may make the judge and the court look bad and, therefore, they should be more discrete.

20. In chambers with counsel for both parties present, a judge politely, but firmly, admonishes a juror for making off-color comments to other jurors about a witness. The admonished juror asks to be excused from jury service, but the judge refuses the request. The juror promptly files a formal complaint about the judge alleging harassment and providing the local newspaper with a copy of the complaint. The judge dismisses the juror from the case and the judge comments to the newspaper that "the allegation is false, and I'll let the proper authorities come to their own conclusions." The judge's comment to the newspaper is:

    a. not allowed under the Code as the only place for comment by the judge is a hearing on the complaint.

    b. allowed under the Code because a judge may directly respond to allegations about the judge's conduct in a matter.

    c. not allowed under the Code because the judge is presiding over the case at the time.

    d. allowed under the Code which requires a judge to maintain order in the court, and the actions by the juror were potentially disruptive to proceedings and needed to be quashed.

21. A judge's drug court is controversial but has proven moderately effective in rehabilitating drug users. The judge's law clerk was a published editor of the law clerk's law school's law review. The law clerk's comment used sound legal reasoning to support the medicinal use of marijuana. While in the court's employment, unbeknownst to the judge, the law clerk authors a widely published article supporting the legalization of drugs and an end to the 'war on drugs'. The law clerk concludes with a commitment to work toward the repeal of restrictive drug laws. The article draws widespread condemnation from law enforcement and prosecutors who have appeared before the judge. The judge:

    a. must respect the law clerk's First Amendment right to freedom of speech as long as the judge does not make such a commitment to work toward the repeal of restrictive drug laws.

    b. must take appropriate action toward the law clerk as the judge must require the court staff, subject to direction and control of the court, to refrain from making prohibited comments such as pledges, promises, or commitments that are inconsistent with the judge's impartial performance of adjudicative duties.

 c. must balance the court's tolerance toward drug users in an attempt to rehabilitate them with the need to maintain an unbiased and neutral court, including court staff.

 d. must step down from the bench for failing to maintain control over the law clerk who made a prohibited statement that has resulted in ill will and reduced trust in the court.

22. A family law judge gets married to an attractive television anchorperson. The wedding is a large social event for members of the bench, bar, and media. At the wedding reception, an attorney, who is known to be a habitual drinker, is clearly intoxicated. In front of a criminal law judge, the attorney makes several inappropriate comments about the young anchorperson. The criminal law judge concurs and also makes a vulgar and disparaging comment about the anchorperson. A third judge, a probate judge, overhears the criminal law judge making the comment. With respect to the comments:

 a. The criminal law judge must take appropriate action with respect to the attorney, and the probate law judge must take appropriate action with respect to the criminal law judge.

 b. Neither the criminal law judge nor the attorney violated any Code with respect to their respective comment or actions as neither were acting in an official capacity.

 c. Given the circumstances and situation, consideration and tolerance should be extended to the judges and lawyers who do not have the same social outlets as persons outside the legal and judicial system.

 d. As the family law judge neither heard, nor was informed of the comments made by the criminal law judge and the attorney, the comments were innocuous and no harm was caused to the judiciary or any attorney. Thus, there was no Code violation.

23. An attorney's temper flares once too often in front of a judge, who slams a gavel onto the bench and holds the attorney in contempt of court. The judge fines the attorney $1,000 and orders the attorney to be held in the county jail for 24 hours "or until cooled off." The attorney's temper erupts again with a string of expletives toward the judge, who then orders the attorney to be held in jail for ten days. The judge has known the attorney for over a decade, but the judge has a duty to maintain order and respect in the court. The prosecutor is the first of several attorneys who file a complaint against the attorney with the state disciplinary agency. When called before the agency to answer questions, the judge, believing the attorney was punished sufficiently, states "the record speaks for itself" and respectfully declines to answer any questions that might jeopardize the attorney's license to practice law. The judge:

 a. acted reasonably by referring the disciplinary agency to a complete record of the incident and knowing other attorneys would answer any questions.

   b. did not violate the Code because the judge presented a full and complete record of the incident to the disciplinary agency for review and has nothing further to add.

   c. violated the Code by sanctioning the attorney with the knowledge that the attorney would also be sanctioned by the disciplinary committee, thereby unjustly punishing the attorney twice for the same conduct.

   d. violated the Code by failing to cooperate with the disciplinary agency.

24. While delivering a brief to the court, an attorney's law clerk sees the judge assigned to the case in the hallway. The law clerk greets the judge and comments that the attorney's client, a criminal defendant, is a childhood friend, a choirboy, and a Rhodes scholar. The judge is annoyed by the law clerk's inappropriate communication. The judge retorts, "that's strange, I thought he was a burglar."

   a. The judge's comment is an ex parte communication in violation of the Code.

   b. The judge's comment is clearly intended as a sarcastic remark toward a non-lawyer and, therefore, is not an ex parte communication.

   c. The law clerk's comment is an ex parte communication that is imparted to the clerk's employer. The attorney has violated the Code.

   d. The law clerk is immune from discipline because the law clerk is not an attorney.

25. Concerned about a complex legal issue relating to state antitrust law, a judge asks for written advice on a point of law from a law school professor with extensive practice experience in the area. The judge makes sure the professor had no connection to any party or attorney in the case. The judge provides all counsel with copies of the correspondence and the professor's response. The judge:

   a. did not violate the Code by consulting the professor as the judge afforded all counsel the opportunity to review communications and to object and respond to the communications.

   b. did not violate the Code as a judge may seek a disinterested expert's advice on the law applicable to a proceeding before the judge.

   c. violated the Code by engaging in an ex parte communication with a disinterested expert without notifying the parties of the person to be consulted and the subject matter to be discussed and providing the parties with a reasonable opportunity to object and respond to the notice and to the advice received.

   d. violated the Code by initiating an ex parte communication with an expert not pre-approved by the parties.

26. A judge, who is nearly deaf without the use of hearing aids, was standing in an office hallway when an attorney in the case about to be heard rushed into the office and began talking to the judge. The judge looked at the attorney and nodded respectfully while the

attorney spoke for several minutes. When the attorney stopped speaking the judge thanked the attorney and motioned to the door. The judge never heard a word the attorney said as the judge's hearing aids were turned off at the time. The judge:

    a. permitted an ex parte communication because the judge knew the attorney was about to be heard in a case before the judge and allowed the attorney to speak outside the presence of the other party or their lawyer.

    b. did not permit an ex parte communication if the judge, after turning the hearing aid on, promptly notified all parties of the incident and afforded them an opportunity to respond.

    c. did not engage in an ex parte communication because the judge heard nothing.

    d. permitted an ex parte communication and, regardless of whether the judge heard the communication, must report the attorney to the appropriate disciplinary authority.

27. In a copyright infringement case, a judge is confused about some of the testimony concerning how a computer program is developed. Not wanting to appear ignorant, the judge searches the internet to learn more about computer programming and even asks a relative, a novice programmer, for some information. The judge:

    a. did not violate the Code because the judge only initiated research after one party opened the door to explaining how computer programs are developed.

    b. violated the Code by independently investigating facts and not considering only the evidence presented and those facts that could be judicially noticed.

    c. violated the Code by not informing all parties and counsel that the judge performed independent research and allowing them to object and respond with their own additional information for consideration.

    d. did not violate the Code as judges have a duty to make informed decisions and ensure a fair trial, even if counsel fails to present sufficient evidence for such an informed decision.

28. A case involving a hostile takeover of a local company with statewide government contracts is before a judge who will retire after the conclusion of the case. The judge, the parties, and the attorneys all know that the judge's great-step-nephew (son of the judge's step-sister's son) is the registered agent and a 10% stockholder in the company. All parties agree that they are comfortable with the judge hearing the case. The judge:

    a. must be disqualified due to the fact that a person within the third degree of relationship to the judge or the judge's spouse is a person with more than a de minimis interest that could be substantially affected by the proceeding.

    b. can hear the case as the judge has made complete disclosure of a familial connection to the proceeding and all parties agree there is no conflict or interest or reason for judicial disqualification.

    c. can hear the case because the great-step-nephew is outside of the judge's immediate family and does not reside in the judge's household.

    d. need not be disqualified as a 10% stock interest, even owned by a person within the judge's immediate household, is only a de minimis interest.

29. If a judge serves as an assistant district attorney prior to ascending to the bench, the judge cannot:

    a. preside over any criminal trial which was filed by the State during the judge's tenure at the District Attorney's office.

    b. hear a case on appeal if it is argued that a member of the District Attorney's office committed malpractice during the judge's tenure at the District Attorney's office.

    c. preside over any criminal trial in which the judge personally handled the motions for continuance filed by the District Attorney's office in the case.

    d. preside over any criminal trial in which the judge was involved in evaluating evidence in the discovery process during the judge's tenure at the District Attorney's office.

30. A judge comes from a rich family. Each of the judge's five children living at home has a trust account established to accommodate gifts from relatives. The judge oversees dozens of stock investments in all of the trusts. The judge:

    a. should appoint an executor to independently oversee the investments so as to avoid any appearance of impropriety and avoid disqualification in a case involving an aspect of the investments or companies in which the children own stock.

    b. must be divested of all responsibility for the stock investments in the trusts because, as the trusts are established for minors, it is really the judge, as a parent, who is in control of the stock.

    c. can invest or oversee investments as an appointment to the bench does not prohibit one from investing wisely.

    d. must make a reasonable effort to keep informed about the personal economic interests of the judge's children who reside in the same household in order to know when the circumstances for disqualification arise.

31. A judge had a clear reason to be disqualified from hearing a probate case because the judge drafted the will of the decedent years earlier. The validity of the will is not being challenged. The judge disclosed the basis for disqualification to counsel in chambers. The judge then asked counsel to leave chambers and consider whether counsel wanted to waive disqualification. The judge's actions were:

    a. in violation of the Code if there was a clear and present possibility that the will may come into contest during the probate proceeding.

b. in accordance with the Code as the judge disclosed the basis for disqualification and asked the lawyers to consider, outside the presence of the judge and court personnel, whether they would agree to waive the judge's disqualification.

c. in violation of the Code if the judge did not present reasons for disqualification in writing to all counsel to allow them an opportunity to respond in writing.

d. in accordance with the Code because the judge is the only judge within a reasonable distance who could hear the case and to allow disqualification would work a hardship on the parties and delay distribution of the proceeds.

32. A judge had a clear reason to be disqualified from acting on a prosecutor's request for an arrest warrant for a violent, convicted felon. The judge was the former defense attorney for the subject of the arrest warrant. The felon was a known flight risk and was seen on video committing an armed robbery. However, no other judge is available, nor could one be available for at least two days. The judge signs the warrant. The judge's actions are:

a. in violation of the Code since the judge should have been disqualified due to having represented the person subject to the warrant.

b. in accordance with the Code since the judge, while subject to disqualification, could be disqualified from any subsequent proceedings at which jeopardy would attach and thereby ensure the defendant's rights were protected.

c. in accordance with the Code since the judge, while subject to disqualification, acted under the rule of necessity because without the warrant there was good reason to believe the subject of the warrant would flee the jurisdiction.

d. in violation of the Code since disqualification under such circumstances is mandatory to protect the attorney-client privilege.

33. A judge can participate in any extrajudicial activity as long as it does not inhibit the judge's ability to independently, fairly, and judiciously conduct the judge's official activities.

a. True. A judge's ability to independently, fairly, and judiciously conduct the affairs of court is the cornerstone of judicial integrity and independence and as long as the judge's conduct does not impede the judge's ability to so act, extrajudicial conduct is allowed.

b. True. Rising to the bench does not require a judge to give up all extrajudicial activities and, in fact, some should be specifically encouraged such as teaching the law.

c. False. There are some extrajudicial activities that are prohibited by law, that interfere with the proper exercise of judicial duties, that lead to frequent disqualification, and that undermine judicial independence, integrity, and impartiality, and such conduct cannot be tolerated.

d. False. Just as the appearance of impropriety is not allowed for judges, the appearance of engaging in extrajudicial activities that may inhibit a judge's ability to independently, fairly, and judiciously conduct the judge's official activities is also prohibited.

34. While giving a public speech to the local League of Women Voters, a judge strongly criticizes recent panels of jurors who, the judge believes, failed to follow the law. The judge contends that these recent jurors failed to recognize that the law requires the prosecutor to bring charges that the jurors may not agree with, but that if the evidence supports a finding of guilt beyond a reasonable doubt, then the oath sworn as a juror gives no choice but to find the defendant guilty. The judge concludes by urging the audience to "keep what I said in mind if you're ever called to jury duty in my court." The judge's choice of words were:
   a. coercive in the mind of a reasonable person and, therefore, had no place in extrajudicial activity.
   b. strongly worded but not likely to overpower the minds of the people listening to a speech outside of the courtroom.
   c. harsh, but it was clear that the judge was simply venting in one of the few available forums to do so.
   d. a reasonable interpretation of the law and subject to interpretation and consideration by any reasonable person.

35. A judge is called upon by a class reunion committee to assist in getting other classmates to attend a reunion, which would also serve as a forum for a 40-minute continuing legal education seminar during a luncheon. The judge agrees and instructs three law clerks to contact a list of attorneys, none of whom ever practiced in front of the judge, to urge them to attend. The judge:
   a. did not violate the Code since the judge made sure none of the attorneys ever practiced in front of the judge.
   b. violated the Code by engaging in extrajudicial activities that made use of court staff or other resources.
   c. did not violate the Code since any attorney who attended the event would engage in continuing legal education which members of the judiciary can support.
   d. violated the Code by contacting licensed attorneys for no purpose relevant to a matter before the court.

36. A probate court judge is concerned about threatened legislative cuts to the funding of state park operations. The judge meets with the chairwoman of the state House of Representatives' Committee on Public Affairs to gain knowledge about the Committee's proposed cuts. During a long meeting, the judge repeatedly advises the chairwoman that cuts to such programs would result in lawsuits by numerous entities and that the judge

finds it difficult to believe any judge would support the proposed actions. The judge points out that the judge would not hear such a suit in probate court. The judge:

    a. violated the Code by using the meeting to determine legislative intent prior to the passage of legislation, thereby giving the judge insider knowledge that could allow the judge to use influence to sway legislation.

    b. did not violate the Code as engaging in information gathering from a public official is not prohibited while on the bench.

    c. did not violate the Code because the judge was acting as a good steward of the environment and, as such, was acting in an allowable fiduciary capacity.

    d. violated the Code by voluntarily consulting with a legislative official.

37. A judge is appointed to an executive branch body that makes recommendations on improvements to the human services system. The body also votes to award grants funded by legislative appropriations, but the judge abstains from all discussions and votes concerning specific grants. The judge's service on the body:

    a. does not violate the Code because the position only indirectly affects the justice system.

    b. violates the Code because the body's purpose does not concern the law, the legal system, or the administration of justice.

    c. violates the Code as appointments to the body are under the control of the executive branch and it is improper for a judge to serve as an appointee from another branch of government.

    d. does not violate the Code because the judge could use the position to award legislative appropriations to fund improvements that may affect the judicial system.

38. A judge may testify as a character witness if:

    a. a judge in a senior court asks the judge to appear before that court to give testimony.

    b. a motion is properly filed with the judge's court, and a hearing is held to determine if the judge has a conflict by testifying. If no conflict exists, the judge may testify.

    c. a legal subpoena has been issued and served upon the judge.

    d. only if a fellow judge requests character witness testimony.

39. A local charity for the poor wants to honor attorneys in the community who serve the indigent on a regular basis. The charity asks a judge for a list of attorneys who have served in a pro bono capacity regularly over the last five years. The judge strongly supports pro bono work and provides to the charity the names of 19 attorneys who meet the criteria. The judge:

    a. did not violate the Code because the judge provided public information acquired in a judicial capacity.

    b. violated the Code by disclosing nonpublic information for a nonjudicial purpose that was acquired in a judicial capacity.

    c. violated the Code by intentionally using judicial office to give preferential recognition to some attorneys over others.

    d. did not violate the Code as recognizing public service is important if the judicial system is to provide equal access to all.

40. For seven generations the Zygmont family has had a living member inducted into the Organizacion Marquee de Guerra, a fraternal organization that raises money for disabled veterans. Judge Zygmont is currently the family member inducted into the organization. The Judge is asked to serve on the organization's Executive Committee. In that capacity, the Judge has reason to review the charter and founding documents. The Judge discovers that the charter limits membership on the Executive Committee to only men, even though women have been members of the organization for two generations. The Judge brings this to the attention of the Committee. Judge Zygmont:

    a. may maintain membership as, despite the document, the organization does not discriminate in its membership.

    b. must resign membership immediately as the organization engages in invidious discrimination that gives rise to the perception that the judge's impartiality is impaired.

    c. may maintain membership but must work to ensure the discriminatory language is removed from all organization documents promptly.

    d. must resign the position on the Executive Committee because the organization's document supports an illegal act, namely, discrimination.

41. A judge belongs to a non-profit charitable organization that raises money for building public parks and has been appointed to its donations committee which is responsible for raising money from the public. The judge:

    a. must resign from the committee because the organization's letterhead lists all committee members.

    b. must resign from the committee as association with it may appear to exert pressure on others to make donations.

    c. may solicit contributions from anyone other than attorneys and parties who have appeared or currently appear in court.

    d. may remain on the committee as long as the judge only solicits contributions from family members or other judges over whom the judge has no authority.

42. A judge of a state's highest court is the only person with the knowledge, education, and

experience, in the judge's family, to serve as guardian for an uncle who suffers from multiple mental and physical disabilities. Without the judge's assistance, the uncle will likely become a ward of the state and be institutionalized. The uncle's expenses are paid from a well-funded trust that has been in litigation by other family members for several years but the judge has steadfastly avoided any participation in the litigation. The judge:

    a. can serve as guardian under a hardship exception to the Code as no other person is willing or able to do so.

    b. can serve as guardian so long as the judge steadfastly continues to avoid any participation in the ongoing litigation.

    c. cannot serve as guardian because the uncle's trust litigation is in a court under the judge's appellate jurisdiction.

    d. cannot serve as guardian due to the fact that the duties will require the judge to act in the best interest of the uncle and regularly take funds from a trust that is under litigation.

43. A local judge, prior to ascending to the bench, was a recognized expert in mediation of high-profile divorce cases. Another judge in a neighboring state is overseeing a messy divorce between movie stars and has asked the local judge to take a few vacation days and mediate the case pro bono. The local judge:

    a. may, at the request of a fellow member of the judiciary, assist with the case.

    b. may not engage in any mediation other than as part of assigned judicial duties.

    c. may never mediate a case because doing so would amount to practicing law.

    d. may mediate the case as it is outside of the state.

44. A judge was a probate lawyer for nearly 20 years prior to ascending to the bench. The judge's younger sister needs a simple will drafted and asks to pay the judge to do it. The judge:

    a. can perform legal work but only for family members that reside within the household.

    b. cannot practice law while an active member of the judiciary.

    c. can perform legal work involving drafting or reviewing legal documents or providing legal advice for family members, but the judge may not accept compensation for such work.

    d. cannot practice law but may accept free legal services for family members from lawyers who do not practice in the judge's court.

45. A judge's family owns a brokerage firm. Family members may invest, trade, and receive services including advice at no cost if they provide any significant service to the family business. The judge regularly attends the firm's management meetings and provides business advice for the firm but does not represent it. The judge manages personal

household financial matters. The judge:

    a. is not violating the Code because the judge's participation and management is in a closely held family business.

    b. is violating the Code by serving in a management capacity of a business interest while sitting on the bench.

    c. is violating the Code by holding and managing the investments of others.

    d. is not violating the Code if the judge fully disclosed involvement prior to being appointed to the bench.

46. A judge's family owns a brokerage firm. Family members may invest, trade, and receive services including advice at no cost if they provide any significant service to the family business. The judge regularly attends the firm's management meetings and provides business advice for the firm but does not represent it. The judge manages personal household financial matters. The judge's brother is the firm's marketing director and aggressively and successfully recruits new business from the legal community and advises them that the judge is a member of the firm. The judge:

    a. may continue involvement with the firm as long as the judge's brother clearly and conspicuously advises potential new clients who are lawyers of the judge's involvement.

    b. may continue involvement with the firm but must keep apprised of all firm clients who are attorneys so the judge may inquire of any potential conflict of interest should an attorney appear before the judge.

    c. may not continue involvement with the firm unless its marketing strategy clearly advises in writing to all attorneys who are potential clients that the judge may be disqualified in their cases if they invest with the firm.

    d. may not continue to participate in or manage the firm's business if such activities will involve the judge with attorneys or other persons likely to come before the court on which the judge serves.

47. A judge is a former Olympic boxer. The judge serves as a referee in Olympic boxing trials and is paid a stipend plus per diem expenses for travels and work around the nation. The judge:

    a. cannot accept compensation for extrajudicial activities as they create a perception that the judiciary is poorly compensated and is subject to bribery.

    b. may not accept compensation if such acceptance would appear to a reasonable person to undermine the judge's independence, integrity, or impartiality.

    c. can only accept a set fee for services to avoid an appearance of padding expenses.

    d. can accept only token compensation and set per diems as allowed under federal law.

48. A judge and the judge's spouse volunteer time over many years to help build a local civic center. The judge and the judge's spouse are offered free season tickets once the civic center is completed. Free season tickets are also offered to a few other key supportive persons and their spouses.
    a. The tickets may be accepted but must be publicly reported.
    b. The tickets may not be accepted unless they are paid for as they have substantial value and very few people were offered free tickets.
    c. The tickets may not be accepted, and the offer must be publicly reported.
    d. The tickets may be accepted, but the judge must pay taxes upon their value.

49. A judge decides a case against a local bank. Two years pass. In need of a second mortgage, the judge applies for and receives a loan from the same bank at a very favorable interest rate. Suspicious, the judge asks a bank officer why the rate was so low and is told it is due to an "exceptional credit score and reputation for honesty." The judge accepts the loan. The judge:
    a. has to report the loan as the bank had an interest that came before the judge in a court.
    b. does not have to report the loan as a similar loan would be given to a person with a similar credit score and reputation.
    c. does not have to report the loan because the judge previously ruled against the bank and could not now be said to have benefitted from an adverse ruling.
    d. has to report the loan to the extent that it is below the published rate afforded to the general public.

50. A judge and the judge's spouse attend a neighboring state's bar association annual weekend meeting. The judge agrees to give a presentation on extradition and waiver at the meeting. While at the weekend conference, the judge and the judge's spouse are wined and dined at several expensive restaurants along with legal product vendors and the neighboring state's bar association officials. The judge and the judge's spouse:
    a. are guests at all the events and could accept the hospitality of their hosts without reservation when they are not allowed to pay their bills.
    b. may accept reimbursement from the neighboring state's bar association but only for actual costs reasonably incurred by the judge and the judge's spouse.
    c. must pay their own way and cannot be reimbursed for expenses incurred at a foreign jurisdiction's events.
    d. may accept reimbursement for the judge's actual costs but not for those of the judge's spouse who was a guest and not a presenter.

51. A judge is a known wine connoisseur and regularly receives a bottle or two of fine wine as a gift or reimbursement. In reporting these things, the judge:

a. complied with the Code if the judge notified the chief judge of the court, in writing, within five business days of receiving the gift or reimbursement and stated what was received, why it was received, and from whom it was received.

b. complied with the Code if the judge filed a public document in court stating the source and activity from which the judge received the wine as a gift or reimbursement but, due to the extensive nature of the judge's wine cellar and its value, the judge did not describe the wine in order to preserve privacy.

c. complied with the Code if the judge filed a report as a public document in court and stated the value of the thing received so that a public record existed for tax reporting and conflict of interest purposes.

d. complied with the Code if the judge filed a report as a public document in court and provided a description of the gift or reimbursement, the activity for which the judge received it, and the source of the reimbursement.

52. A judge must make required public reports about reimbursement of expenses and waiver of fees or charges:

a. at least bi-annually but within 60 days of the event or program for which the judge received a reimbursement or waiver.

b. always within 30 days of the event or program for which the judge received a reimbursement or waiver.

c. always within 60 days of the event or program for which the judge received a reimbursement or waiver.

d. at least annually.

JUDICIAL CONDUCT

ANSWERS TO REVIEW QUESTIONS

Answer 1

The correct answer is choice A. The Model Code of Judicial Conduct's first canon requires a judge to uphold and promote the judiciary's independence, integrity, and impartiality.

Answer 2

The correct answer is choice C. A judge acts impartially if the judge has a lack of prejudice or bias in favor of, or against a party, as well as an open mind about all issues that come before the court.

Answer 3

The correct answer is choice C. Any conduct that adversely affects public confidence in the judiciary is considered an impropriety.

Answer 4

The correct answer is choice B. A judge's conduct creates an appearance of impropriety if the conduct would create in reasonable minds a perception that the judge violated the Code or engaged in other conduct that reflects negatively on the judge's impartiality, honesty, temperament, or fitness.

Answer 5

The correct answer is choice C. A judge must not allow others to abuse the prestige of judicial office in order to advance their personal or economic interests.

Answer 6

The correct answer is choice A. Purchasing used furniture, albeit expensive and from a retiring partner of a local law firm, if offered for sale to the public, advances neither the personal nor economic interests of the judge or others and, therefore, is not an abuse of the prestige of judicial office.

Answer 7

The correct answer is choice D. A judge's judicial duties take precedence over all his other activities, and to ensure he can perform his duties he must conduct any extrajudicial and personal activities so as to reduce the risk of conflict or disqualification.

Answer 8

The correct answer is choice C. A judge must uphold and apply the law while performing judicial duties fairly and impartially. A judge must manifest objectivity and open-mindedness regardless of whether the judge approves of the law in question.

Answer 9

The correct answer is choice C. While a judge must perform duties without bias, prejudice, or harassment with respect to race, gender, sex, religion, ethnicity, national origin, disability, age, marital status, sexual orientation, political affiliation, or socioeconomic status, a judge may make legitimate references to factors when they are pertinent to an issue in the case.

Answer 10

The correct answer is choice B. A judge must not permit court officials, court staff, or others subject to the judge's direction and control to manifest bias or prejudice, to engage in harassment, including but not limited to bias, prejudice, or harassment based on race, gender, sex, religion, ethnicity, national origin, disability, age, marital status, sexual orientation, political affiliation, or socioeconomic status.

Answer 11

The correct answer is choice B. Judges must decide cases based on the law and facts, regardless of whether the laws or facts are unpopular or popular. Similarly, judges should not be swayed by public clamor or fear of criticism, nor should they allow family or financial relationships or interests to influence their official conduct or judgment.

Answer 12

The correct answer is choice A. A judge must not allow social or other relationships or interests to influence the judge's judicial conduct or judgment.

Answer 13

The correct answer is choice A. In order to ensure that judges are available to do their judicial duties, they must conduct their extrajudicial and personal activities so as to reduce the risk of conflicts that would result in disqualification from participating in proceedings. Judges are not required to refrain from participating in or supporting a religious institution of their choice, However, they must reduce the risk of conflicts such participation or support may cause.

Answer 14

The correct answer is choice C. A judge must perform administrative and judicial duties competently and diligently as well as supervise and monitor cases in ways that eliminate or reduce dilatory practices, avoidable delays, and unnecessary costs. By ignoring a known administrative personnel problem under the judge's control that has delayed cases, added to costs, and diminished the decorum and demeanor of the court, the judge has violated the Code.

Answer 15

The correct answer is choice D. A judge must provide the parties to a legal proceeding with the right to be heard, but a judge may also encourage, without coercion, parties and their lawyers to settle disputed matters, and the judge may participate in a settlement discussion. However, a judge must also consider the effect participation in a settlement discussion may have on the judge's objectivity and impartiality. Here, the judge offered to hear the parties, including their discrete matters, in chambers, in an effort to settle the case. The judge only offered to consider the case if any party made such a motion after the attempt to settle the case failed. Such an offer does not amount to coercion.

Answer 16

The correct answer is choice B. A judge must hear and decide matters that come before the court unless the Code or law requires disqualification to protect the rights of litigants and preserve public confidence in the judiciary's independence, integrity, and impartiality. A judge should not use disqualification to avoid matters that involve difficult, unpopular, or controversial issues.

Answer 17

The correct answer is choice C. A judge must maintain order and decorum in all proceedings before the judge.

Answer 18

The correct answer is choice D. A judge must be patient, dignified, and courteous to jurors, litigants, witnesses, lawyers, court officials, court staff, and others with whom the judge deals in an official capacity. This includes persons who may not share the judge's or the judicial system's values or traditions.

Answer 19

The correct answer is choice C. Certain restrictions on judicial speech are essential to the maintenance of the judiciary's independence, integrity, and impartiality with regard to pending and impending matters before the court. A judge must not make any statement that might substantially interfere with a fair trial or hearing. The judge must also require court staff and others subject to the judge's direction and control to refrain from making statements that the judge would be prohibited from making.

Answer 20

The correct answer is choice B. While a judge may not make a public statement that might reasonably be expected to impair the fairness of or affect the outcome of a pending or impending matter, a judge may respond to allegations about the judge's conduct in a matter.

Answer 21

The correct answer is choice B. The judge must require that court staff, court officials, and others subject to the judge's direction and control act in a way consistent with the judge's duties pursuant to the Code, including the prohibition on making comments such as pledges, promises, or commitments that are inconsistent with the judge's impartial performance of adjudicative duties.

Answer 22

The correct answer is choice A. A judge must take appropriate action when the judge has a reasonable belief that the performance of another judge or lawyer is impaired by alcohol, drugs, or an emotional, mental, or physical condition. Appropriate action may include a confidential referral to an assistance program. The attorney's apparent alcohol problem should give the criminal law judge reasonable belief that the attorney may be impaired. A judge having knowledge that another judge has committed a violation of the Code that raises a substantial question about the other judge's trustworthiness, honesty, or fitness for judicial office must inform the appropriate authority.

Answer 23

The correct answer is choice D. A judge must cooperate and be honest and candid with lawyer and judicial disciplinary agencies.

Answer 24

The correct answer is choice A. Subject to certain exceptions, a judge must not initiate, permit, or consider ex parte communications, or consider other communications made to the judge outside the presence of the parties regarding an impending or pending matter. The rule applies to communications with people other than the proceeding's participants, such as law teachers and other attorneys.

Answer 25

The correct answer is choice C. A judge may only obtain the advice of a disinterested expert on the law applicable to a proceeding before the court if the judge: (1) notifies the parties of the person to be consulted and the subject matter to be discussed; and (2) provides the parties a reasonable opportunity to object and respond to the notice and to the advice received.

Answer 26

The correct answer is choice C. An ex parte communication is a communication made to a judge for or by one party outside the presence of the other party. A critical element is missing here, namely, communication, which requires the judge to have heard what the attorney said outside the presence of opposing counsel. The judge could not consider what could not be heard.

Answer 27

The correct answer is choice B. A judge may not investigate facts in a matter independently. The judge must consider only the evidence presented and those facts that may properly be judicially noticed.

Answer 28

The correct answer is choice A. A judge must be disqualified from any participation in a proceeding in which the judge's impartiality might reasonably be questioned. A judge's duty not to hear or decide matters in which disqualification is required applies whether or not a party files a motion to disqualify the judge. Impartiality might reasonably be questioned if a person within a third degree of relationship to the judge or the judge's domestic partner/spouse is a person with more than a de minimis interest that could be substantially affected by the proceeding.

Answer 29

The correct answer is choice D. A judge must be disqualified from any participation in a proceeding in which the judge's impartiality might reasonably be questioned. If the judge previously served as a prosecutor, and in that capacity participated substantially and personally as a lawyer regarding the proceeding, the judge's impartiality might reasonably be questioned.

Answer 30

The correct answer is choice D. A judge must make a reasonable effort to keep informed about the personal economic interests of the judge's domestic partner or spouse and minor children residing in the judge's household in order to know when the judge must be disqualified from participation in a proceeding.

Answer 31

The correct answer is choice B. A judge who is subject to disqualification, other than for bias or prejudice, may disclose the basis of the judge's disqualification and ask the parties and their lawyers to consider, outside the presence of the judge and court personnel, if they will waive disqualification.

Answer 32

The correct answer is choice C. The general rule of disqualification is subject to exceptions and may be overridden due to necessity.

Answer 33

The correct answer is choice C. Although a judge may participate in extrajudicial activities, there are some extrajudicial activities that are prohibited by law, that interfere with the proper exercise of judicial duties, that lead to frequent disqualification, and that undermine judicial independence, integrity, and impartiality, and such conduct cannot be tolerated.

Answer 34

The correct answer is choice A. When participating in extrajudicial activities, a judge may not engage in conduct that would appear to a reasonable person to be coercive.

Answer 35

The correct answer is choice B. When engaging in extrajudicial activities, a judge must not make use of court staff, premises, equipment, stationary, or other resources, except for incidental use for activities that concern the legal system, the law, or the administration of justice.

Answer 36

The correct answer is choice D. Generally, a judge must not appear voluntarily at a public hearing or otherwise consult with executive or legislative officials or bodies.

Answer 37

The correct answer is choice B. A judge must not accept appointment to a governmental committee, commission, board, or other governmental position unless the position concerns the law, the legal system, or the administration of justice.

Answer 38

The correct answer is choice C. Only if a judge is duly summoned may the judge testify as a character witness in an administrative, judicial, or other adjudicatory proceeding. Testifying as a character witness without a subpoena abuses the prestige of judicial office in order to advance someone else's interest.

Answer 39

The correct answer is choice A. A judge must not intentionally disclose or use, for any purpose unrelated to the judge's judicial duties, nonpublic information acquired in a judicial capacity. However, the information requested here is a matter of public record.

Answer 40

The correct answer is choice B. A judge's membership in an organization that engages in invidious discrimination gives rise to perceptions that the judge's impartiality is impaired and the judge must immediately resign from such an organization upon learning of the same.

Answer 41

The correct answer is choice D. Generally, judges may engage in non-profit educational, religious, charitable, fraternal, or civic extrajudicial activities, even when such activities do not involve the law. The judge may solicit contributions only from family members or other judges over whom the judge lacks authority.

Answer 42

The correct answer is choice C. A judge cannot serve in a fiduciary position when a trust, estate, or ward for which the judge is responsible becomes involved in adversary proceedings in the court on which the judge serves, or another court under its appellate jurisdiction.

Answer 43

The correct answer is choice B. A judge may not act as an arbitrator or a mediator or perform other judicial functions separate from the judge's official duties. However, a judge may participate in arbitration, mediation, or settlement conferences conducted as part of assigned judicial duties.

Answer 44

The correct answer is choice C. A judge may not practice law. However, a judge may, without compensation, provide legal advice to, and draft or review documents for, a member of the judge's family.

Answer 45

The correct answer is choice A. A judge may not serve as a director, officer, manager, general partner, employee, or advisor of any business entity. However, a judge may participate or manage in a business closely held by the judge or member of the judge's family or a business entity mainly involved in investment of the judge's financial resources and those of the judge's family members.

Answer 46

The correct answer is choice D. A judge may not engage in management of business entities if their financial activities will involve the judge in frequent transactions or continuing business relationships with lawyers or other persons likely to come before the court on which the judge serves.

Answer 47

The correct answer is choice B. A judge may not accept compensation if such acceptance would appear to a reasonable person to undermine the judge's independence, integrity, or impartiality.

Answer 48

The correct answer is choice A. A judge must report accepted invitations to a judge and spouse to attend without charge an event connected with the judge's civic activities if the identical invitation is given to nonjudges who are involved in that activity in similar ways as the judge.

Answer 49

The correct answer is choice A. A judge must report accepted gifts, loans, bequests, benefits, or